SONG OF
Massacre at Sand Creek
SORROW

Patrick M. Mendoza

Willow Wind Publishing Company
P.O. Box 6159
Denver, Colorado 80206

Published by Willow Wind Publishing Company
P.O. Box 6159
Denver, Colorado 80206

Manufactured in the United States of America

Cover Artwork by David Bowman

Cheyenne Woman in Cover Artwork: Ann Strange Owl

Library of Congress Catalogue Card Number: 93-93930

ISBN: 0-9636362-0-0

1   2   3   4   5   6   7   8   9   10

Dedication

In Loving Memory of:
My Father and Mother.
And to the memory of the
Tsis Tsis Tas' lodge fires of old:
May they forever burn warm
in the hearts of "The People."

Acknowledgments

Writing the acknowledgments of this book was the hardest part, because I was afraid I might forget someone. Without the help of those numerous people of very diversified backgrounds who talked to me for hours during my research, this book would not have been possible.

First of all I would like to thank Mary Joy Martin, author and artist from Montrose, Colorado, for inspiring the song I wrote about the Sand Creek Massacre and Douglas McQuide, editor of *The Comstock Quarterly*, wherever he is, for initially talking me into writing this book after he read and published a short story I wrote for that magazine. From *The Comstock Quarterly* my journey took me to the offices of then U. S. Congressman (now U. S. Senator) Ben Nighthorse Campbell who taught me my first lesson of Tsis Tsis Tas etiquette and introduced me to Ann Strange Owl, great-granddaughter of George Bent and Magpie, who taught me the first words in her language I was able to speak. I would also like to thank Henry Lowenstein of the Denver Civic Theatre for introducing me to Richard Tall Bull.

From Colorado my journey took me to Bent's Fort near La Junta, Colorado and to "Alex" the head ranger and Craig Moore who allowed me to sleep inside the old fort in the same fashion of those 150 years before me. From Colorado my journey in search of this book took me to Oklahoma numerous times to Lucille Bent, granddaughter of George Bent, Robert and June Prairie Chief, Marcella Panana, and to my Cheyenne brother, John Sipes and his mother Cleo who has been my linguistics teacher.

I would also like to thank Tom Noel, Ph.D., from the University of Colorado Denver Center and Donald Berthrong, Ph.D.,

Purdue University, for taking time to spend a long Sunday with me in West Lafayette, Indiana.

Chapter two would have been void of the beauty of the plains without Jennifer Slater, wildlife biologist, Colorado Department of Wildlife, Lamar, Colorado. Thank you for the descriptions of the wildlife and vegetation in the 1820's. And many thanks to Russ Rigtrup of the Forney Transportation Museum of Denver for information on John Evans' route from Chicago to Denver in 1862.

To Rosemary Fetter of Metropolitan State College, many thanks for Mother Maggard and for the great afternoons at the Wynkoop Brewery with the rest of the gang. And to my friends Paul Hanway for the traditional Arapaho tales and to Sawyer Tom Hayden, great-great-grandson of John Evans and one great cowboy poet and singer.

No research project can be completed with out the dedication of the many historians who live their work in historic societies, like Mary Payne of the Warren County Historic Society who placed John Evans and John Chivington within ten miles of each other for me, and the folks of the Wyoming State Historical Museum, the Colorado Historic Society and The Denver Public Library Western History Division. Many special thanks to my friend Sonny Reisch, at Fort Phil Kearney, Wyoming, for the papers and letters of William Fetterman. And special thanks Bea Rader, Ph.D., Colorado folklorist extraordinaire of the Arvada Center for the Performing Arts, for introducing me to Neva Standing Bear-Light-In-The-Lodge and to Connie Buffalo for the last chapter of this book. I also wish to thank Virginia Cole Trenholm who will be ninety-one years old in March of 1993. She is the foremost living authority on the history of the Arapaho and Shoshonis peoples, people she's lived with and loved for over fifty years. She gave me my Arapaho name of "Haw Thee Day Hee" — the Storyteller. To Ruthie Mendoza, my sister-in-law and proof reader, "ah ho bah." And last but not least, to Dona, my best friend and wife, who wouldn't let me quit at the beginning and who put up with a bunch, while this book was being written over and over and over again.

Patrick M. Mendoza
November 29, 1992

Contents

U.S. Senator Ben Nighthorse Campbell, great-grandson of Black Horse

Photo courtesy U.S. Senator Campbell's office

Foreword

The spirits speak to you there, at Sand Creek; they truly do. You can hear them as the wind rustles the trees, in the call of the birds. Other than that, it's mostly a quiet place. You would almost want to say it's a peaceful place, except that is not possible when you understand what happened there.

Song of Sorrow eloquently tells the story of what happened to the Arapahoe and the Cheyenne people at Sand Creek. It leads us gently, yet ominously into a tale we know does not end well: the story of one of the most infamous massacres of innocent Indian people during the so-called "settling" of the West.

Author, Pat Mendoza does a brilliant job of bringing the reader into the story, of making you feel, hear and see what occurred. The reader feels the story in the gut and it is a soul-stirring experience. But, more than learning only what happened, you find out who it happened to, how it happened and why it happened.

As a person of Indian ancestry, I particularly appreciate Pat Mendoza's ability to set the scene and lead the reader into the complex Indian culture that existed on the Great Plains in the 19th century. My ancestors come to life under Mendoza's pen and I feel as if I actually get to meet them, to know their hopes, their fears and feelings.

But, that didn't save my relatives from Col. Chivington and his militia. These people were caught up in that horrible tragedy. They were raped, killed and tortured and we can't go back now and save them. But, with Mendoza's help, we can remember them and honor them.

For Indian people do not restrict the honor accorded our ancestors despite vast distances or time that has passed. And our

cultures; half-siblings, in-laws and distant cousins become as sisters and brothers in our cultural realms.

I trace my Cheyenne heritage to Black Horse, who road with Two Moons in the Battle at Little Bighorn up in Montana. Black Horse had three wives, and I have been told that one of these was the daughter of one of Black Kettle's sisters. They say this ancestor, Yellow Woman, was raped at Sand Creek, but survived. A Southern Cheyenne named Jasper Red Hat has told me that his branch of our people believes my great-grandmother may have died at Sand Creek.

It is difficult for me to know exactly who my ancestors were or what happened to them, precisely because of the unspeakable horrors that happened during the "Indian wars" of the 1800's, and because our people passed historical knowledge of our tribe and culture through an oral tradition; we had no written language. So, you hear stories that someone else heard from someone else around a campfire one night, but you never really know for sure.

What I do know for sure is the incredible sorrow and loss I feel at Sand Creek. Even a bright, sunny day seems subdued. But, I am comforted by the voices of the spirits I hear there. They are still with me.

Song of Sorrow tells this story of years ago so well it brings you there, allowing the reader to feel and hear those spirits at the banks of Sand Creek, too.

UNITED STATES SENATOR BEN NIGHTHORSE CAMPBELL
(Northern Cheyenne)

Introduction

Though history is my avocation, for the past fifteen years I have been making my living as a storyteller and singer. During this time, while reading the volumes of historic literature I've used to create my stories and songs, one incident in Colorado history would not leave my mind, it was the story of the Sand Creek Massacre.

Most of the history texts and related articles I read all dealt with the dates and events leading to the slaughter of the Cheyenne and Arapaho on November 29, 1864. As a storyteller, I wondered about the actual thoughts and feelings of all the people involved. In 1986, I unknowingly began this book with a song I wrote for one of my concerts. The reaction the song had on my listeners amazed me, so I began to take a much closer look at this historic incident known as "the Sand Creek Massacre."

In 1989, three years after I had written my song, I wrote a short story about Sand Creek for the now defunct magazine, *The Comstock Quarterly*. The editor, Mr. Doug McQuide contacted me some weeks later and suggested I write a full length book. He thought the idea of a storyteller writing history was a unique approach. After thousands of miles of travel between the lands of the Northern and Southern Cheyenne and hundreds of hours of listening to the traditional oral tales and interviewing leading historians on the Cheyenne and Arapaho, such as Donald Berthrong of Purdue University and Virginia Cole Trenholm, what follows is a very different approach to history. Much of the information herein has existed for many years, but to my knowledge, this book contains never before published material and photos.

Although this book reads like a novel, it is unfortunately non-fiction. As this book hits the shelves in retail stores, tales similar to

Sand Creek are continuing to happen throughout the world: Yugoslavia, Somalia and countries like Germany being torn apart by bigotry and hate with its rise of neo-Nazis brutalizing and killing "foreigners."

As a former warrior, I have learned that if you can teach a person to hate, you can teach a person to kill. It is done every day in every military boot camp around the world. And that hatred takes many forms: skin color, religion, sexual preference, tribal names and any other reason one can find for mankind's differences.

As a storyteller, I've become a listener to all races and religions and I have learned to share stories with my world's cohabitating humans instead of bullets. There is magic in the spoken and written word, no matter the language, if we would only take time to listen.

Patrick M. Mendoza
Denver, Colorado
November 29, 1992

1
The Tsis Tsis Tas

The Great Spirit made the earth
With wind and sun and rain,
And out of all things
Came birth and love and pain.

On the last night of Yellow Wolf's life, no one knew what the old chief may have dreamed. Could he have dreamed of the time when more than just a trickle of water flowed down the bed of Big Sandy Creek and the buffalo herds were so vast it took days for them to cross one given point on the plains? Or did the old chief dream of summers past when his bones didn't ache with the age of his eighty-five years? No one knows. He may have dreamed of times when cottonwood trees and juniper sang summer's song of essence. Filled with life, the Cheyenne summer sang a chorus echoed by the rugged beauty of a land perfumed with sweet sage, its melody orchestrated by miles of waving prairie grass. And warm soothing winds swept onto this great prairie like a resonant quilt, after winter's harshness faded into the fickleness of spring. Maybe Old Yellow Wolf dreamed of those times when his people roamed this land without sighting a white man. Yellow Wolf did recall in the white man's year of 1806, Zebulon Pike and his white warriors came from eastern lands. This tribe of whites spoke a different tongue than had the Spaniards, who roamed the area for years. It made the old chief think about how they, the Cheyenne, were named from a Lakota word.

As a young boy, Yellow Wolf and other Cheyenne children often sat around the crackling warmth of village camp fires and

1

listened intently to old men talk about his tribe's traditions and lore, how they called themselves, "Tsis Tsis Tas,"[1] which in the Algonquin language means, "people alike," or "our people." In the days of Yellow Wolf's grandfather's grandfather, before the Tsis Tsis Tas possessed horses, so the stories said, they lived farther north near a huge, great lake and later near a vast river they called Missouri (Algonquin—meaning "People of the Big Canoes"). When white expansion forced the Tsis Tsis Tas to make their exodus from this land, they met another tribe of Indians called Lakota. Because neither tribe understood the language of the other, the Tsis Tsis Tas were called "Shai ena,"[2] which in Lakota meant, "people speaking a strange tongue." Since that time other tribes and eventually the white man adopted Shai ena or Cheyenne for Tsis Tsis Tas.

The old ones told those young wide-eyed listeners, the Tsis Tsis Tas once lived during a "golden age." It was a time before the horse and a thing called "war." In this "golden age" all men and strangers were greeted in peace as they warmed themselves by the village fires. With the coming of the horse however, life changed for the Tsis Tsis Tas. This animal became the most sought after possession on the Great Plains. Utilization of the horse gave the Tsis Tsis Tas, and other tribes, a mobility they'd never before experienced. In fact, the Tsis Tsis Tas, like most plains Indians, became superb horsemen. With this new, speedy mode of transportation, the Tsis Tsis Tas lost their golden age. Warfare replaced peace as this verdant grassland's greatest splendor.

Warfare to the Tsis Tsis Tas and other Indian tribes was not the brutal slaughter of an entire enemy. Great losses of life were rare in tribal fighting. Sporadic incidents of chance meetings, or a planned raid designed to quench revenge's thirst constituted a great battle to the Plains Indians. Most importantly, war to the Tsis Tsis Tas was the actual love of combat. The coming of the white man though taught the Tsis Tsis Tas the lessons of wholesale slaughter.

In growing up, Yellow Wolf may have remembered how he and the other boys were taught the fundamental skills of being warriors and hunters. In his mind, he could still feel his muscles cramping from the hours he stood absolutely motionless while stalking game or enemy. Stealth and cunning were instilled in males at an early

[1]Pronounced "Tah Tees Tahs" or "Geez Geez Tahs," depending on Northern or Southern dialect.
[2]*The Cheyenne Indians* by George Bird Grinnell, p. 3.

age. With few exceptions, all became warriors. Yet Yellow Wolf and the other Tsis Tsis Tas were taught "counting coup" in battle signified the most valiant warriors.

Counting coup involved a warrior riding up to an enemy brave and striking him with a lance or stick without killing him. His memory brought back the chase's pure exhilaration; the fight's excitement stirred the fires of Yellow Wolf's mind as he recalled charging an armed enemy and escaping with life and limb intact. He remembered other legendary accounts of counting coup. Once in a fight with some Pawnee, nine Tsis Tsis Tas counted coup on one warrior. The Pawnee left the battle alive, though bruised, battered and very sore.

Yellow Wolf became mythic with his many acts of not killing anyone. Taking a life held no honor for him. As a member of the "Rope Throwers" clan, Yellow Wolf's special talent lay in stealing enemy horses. It helped make him a chief. Old Big Foot, another member of the clan, was also noted for his ability to steal horses. The Tsis Tsis Tas told stories of how Big Foot once used a lasso to pull a fleeing Ute from his horse, claiming yet another four-legged prize.

Young warriors learned the arts of hunting and warfare, but the old ones enlightened all Tsis Tsis Tas about their creation. They were told water once covered the earth and a great warrior fell from the sky into the flood. As he floated on the surface, he beckoned all of the waterfowl to him and commanded them to dive beneath the waters to search for mother earth. The swans and geese tried many times but each failed. Then a little duck appeared. He took a deep breath and disappeared deep below the water. He did not return for a long time and the great warrior decided he surely must have drowned. But then he noticed the duck's appearance above the water's surface and what appeared to be mud on its bill. This small water fowl had found earth. After the mud dried, the wind swept it away and spread it into land forms we now call earth's continents. And from that soft earth, man and woman were formed. They were called Summer and Winter. Their struggles on earth produced other climatic and seasonal changes. The sun was their joy, rain their sorrow and the icy winds represented their anger.

And of their deities, Yellow Wolf learned his people called the great spirit of the sky "Heammawihio,"[3] The Wise One Above.

---

[3] *The Cheyenne Indians*, p. 88. Pronounced "Hay Ahmma Mahay oh."

Below earth, there lived another benevolent spirit, whom his people named "Ahk tun o' wihio,"[4] The Wise One Below. He possessed powers similar to Heammawihio. And in the winds of the earth, there were four powerful spirits who dwelled at the four points of the compass.

To pay homage to their gods, the Tsis Tsis Tas created a ceremonial pipe made from red sandstone. They used it in all ceremonies they held sacred, and in smoking, Yellow Wolf and others would always offer puffs of smoke to these six deities: first to the sky and earth, then to the winds of the east, south, west, and north. Heammawihio was the chief god and creator, and in pipe ceremonies, the Tsis Tsis Tas always offered the stem to him before all others. Then they offered it to earth's great power. Yellow Wolf implored Ahk tun o' wihio to make everything grow, so food might be bountiful and all would live. He prayed the rivers and waters would flow so all might drink and not suffer from thirst. And he prayed the grass would grow, for his animals needed nourishment from the land. Then, he prayed for the plants and herbs of medicine, so his people might heal themselves when ill.

After reverently offering the pipe to these great spirits, the Tsis Tsis Tas offered its stem to the four directions, praying to the gods who dwelled there to calm the winds so their lodges would stay firmly on the ground. The east was always offered the first smoke, for all life arises from the land where "the sun comes out of the ground."[5] Then the pipe is offered to the south wind, because it is from there the warm winds originate. The pipe is then offered to the west wind, for all of life rests in the land where the sun "goes back into the earth." Lastly, but never irreverently, the smoke is offered to the north wind, it is there the winter dwells. For in this land of the Great Plains, the winds blew more fiercely than anywhere else in North America with the exception of the ocean shores. At times, winds here equaled a hurricane's ferocity. Yellow Wolf believed fervently in his deities because many times within minutes he saw perfectly calm days with infinite visibility change into blinding walls of rain or snow. He had also seen extreme temperature changes brought on by the wind, when warm summer-like days turned to freezing cold without warning. Yellow Wolf felt it wise always to pray to all of the gods, in one's own way. Yet, his people

[4]*The Cheyenne Indians*, p. 88. Also personal interviews with Ann Strange Owl and Lucille Bent. Pronounced "Ahk tun o'mahay oh."
[5]Cheyenne folklore.

criticized no one for their fervency in faith or lack of it. Religion was personal for these nomads of the plains.

The old ones told other stories to Yellow Wolf and the other children. One of the most intriguing told of Heammawihio's arrival on earth and how he lived amongst the Tsis Tsis Tas. The old chief's memory may have drifted back to those days of youth and he may have smiled at his thoughts. How wonderful it would have been to have lived when the Wise One Above taught his people how to make spearheads from stone. From bone and stone, Heammawihio taught the Tsis Tsis Tas how to make knives for cutting meat and skin. Yellow Wolf must have thought of the honor it would have been to be the first of his people to be taught how to make bows and arrows by this great spirit. The Wise One Above also taught the Tsis Tsis Tas buffalo, elk, deer and earth's other animals were to be hunted for food and clothing. He taught the Tsis Tsis Tas to pray over those animals and thank them for their sacrifice. Staring at the fire's flickering embers, Yellow Wolf could only have imagined the excitement of his people when Heamma-wihio taught them fire's secret. He informed the Tsis Tsis Tas that rubbing two sticks together at great speed created heat. The heat's acceleration then created a small flame. And he shared the secret of the two special stones, which, when swiftly struck together, caused sparks. He taught them about fire's benefit, so they might cook their food and stay warm during cold nights.

Sometimes, Old Yellow Wolf could have felt himself a little touched in the head when he thought these things. On the other hand, he may have wondered if all men dreamed of being alive when gods roamed the earth, of hearing their words and of personally learning from them.

The old chief might have wondered how The Wise One Above sounded when he told the Tsis Tsis Tas they were not alone in this world, for he had created other people, different from them, whom they would one day meet. And he may have wondered what his people felt knowing The Wise One Above gave these other persons the same gifts of fire, arrows and knives. Old Yellow Wolf could only guess how the great Wise One Above instructed the Tsis Tsis Tas to plant, grow and cultivate corn from the earth. Was his voice sooth-ing and gentle or was The Wise One Above's voice deep and commanding? He was glad his people remembered Heamma-wihio's warning; one day other humans from a strange, powerful land would cross the big water and meet the Tsis Tsis Tas. And

Chief Yellow Wolf of the Hair Rope Clan. Drawn from life by Lt. J. W. Abert, 1846, U.S. Army.
Courtesy Colorado Historic Society

there would be war as they had never known, and many would die.

    After this great spirit taught the Tsis Tsis Tas these lessons, he stayed with them a long time, before returning to the sky. Before leaving, Heammawihio said he would always look after "Our People." When they died, he promised the Tsis Tsis Tas a never ending life with him. He told them their life on earth would always be filled with troubles. The Wise One Above told his people he called his home in the sky "Seyan"[6] and all who died — the good, the bad, the brave and the cowardly — would go to this place. For in the sky's world, there was no "reward for virtue or punishment for sin."[7] Only those people who killed themselves would not be allowed in Seyan. The only way the spirit, or "tasoom,"[8] reached

[6] *The Cheyenne Indians*, p. 91
[7] Ibid., p. 93.
[8] Ibid., p. 93.

Seyan after death was to cross the four great rivers and follow the sky across the Milky Way. And in that place, the Tsis Tsis Tas would live much the same way as on earth, except game was always plentiful and illness did not exist.

On the last day of his life, Old Yellow Wolf may have thought about those times and places. But his people's reality, since the time of his birth, were the thousands of white men coming to their land. Some of those men were good, but many respected neither Yellow Wolf's people nor their land. However, he knew of their coming long before their arrival. He remembered the prophecies of one called Sweet Medicine.

Long ago, tribal elders told stories about this prophet, how he came amongst the Tsis Tsis Tas before they owned horses. In the years of his grandfather's grandfather, they related, there lived a maiden in a Tsis Tsis Tas village. Her father and mother were middle-aged and good people. It was said her father's strength enabled him to outrun and outthrow the village's young men. And the elders spoke of her mother as a very gracious woman.

One night the maiden heard a voice calling to her in the night saying, "Sweet Root will come to you, because you are clean and a young woman."[9] So vivid was her dream, the girl went to her mother the following morning and told her of it. Her mother reassured her it was only a dream. But the girl's vision returned the next night and two nights thereafter. Each time she told her mother, she was comforted and reminded it was just a dream. It became more vivid though, with each night's experience, as the voice called to her, "Sweet Root will come to you, because you are clean and a young woman."

One day, four months later, the young girl discovered she was with child. This could not be, for she had never been with a man! When her parents learned of her condition, they were ashamed. As hard as the girl tried to explain, her story was not believed. The girl and her parents did what they could to hide her problem from the rest of the village. Five months later, on the day she gave birth to the child, she went to a river bank. Hiding in some high grass, she delivered this child of mysterious conception. She left her newborn infant in the high grass and ran back to her village, never to see the child again.

---

[9] *Cheyenne Memories*, p. 27.

Not long after, an old woman from another village came down to the river to collect rye grass. She and others of her people used the grass as a cushion beneath the buffalo robes on which they slept. Using an antelope shaft as a knife, she began cutting the grass. But she heard movement along the river bank. Silently she scanned the area for signs of danger. Her vigil was broken only by the sound of an infant's cry. Without hesitation, she rushed to where the child was lying. When she saw this helpless, abandoned newborn, she gently picked him up and cradled him close to her breast. The old woman put aside her task of cutting grass, wrapped the child up and took him home. Upon returning to her village, she took the child into her lodge and told her husband, "Old man I have found a baby that someone has thrown away."[10]

Her husband rose up from his seated position and praised his wife and the Wise One Above for their good fortune. As he raised the child in his arms towards Seyan, he exclaimed, "This is our grandson and his name shall be Sweet Medicine."[11] As happy as they were at this moment though, the old man and woman in their wildest dreams could not imagine why anyone would desert a newborn baby, as this was not their way.

The old woman took the boy to some mothers of her village still with young children. He was nursed and loved by those young mothers. It came to pass, Sweet Medicine matured quickly, and as a child of ten, performed his first miracle. During this time, before the Tsis Tsis Tas had horses, a terrible drought caused the buffalo herds to roam farther south to greener grasslands. Sweet Medicine's people hungered and were too weak to follow the herds. So the ten-year-old prophet asked his mother to find him a long cherrywood bough. Sweet Medicine fashioned the bough into a hoop and tied it together with thread made of sinew. He then requested the younger women of the village to weave him a net of buckskin, leaving a hole in the middle. Sweet Medicine then tied this net to the cherrywood bough. Cutting a piece of hide from an old buffalo robe, the young prophet shaped it into a ball and asked the men and boys to throw it through his odd hoop. Although thinking him slightly mad for wanting to play this silly game in a time of famine, they tried, but failed. At last, Sweet Medicine took his turn to throw the ball. His aim was true and as the robe exited the other side of the hoop, it was transformed into a living buffalo calf.

---

[10]Ibid., p. 28.
[11]Ibid., p. 28.

This miracle and stories of Sweet Medicine's exile and return were told to Yellow Wolf and his friends by the old ones. They also learned of how Sweet Medicine brought the Sacred Medicine Arrows and laws that governed his people. More astounding, as his life ebbed towards his eighty-fifth year, Yellow Wolf witnessed the fulfillment of Sweet Medicine's prophecies.

From the time he and the Tsis Tsis Tas before him could remember, the Keepers of the Sacred Medicine Arrows related the tale of Sweet Medicine's final days. The Prophet gathered his people around him in his last hours of life and said,

> There is a time coming, though, when many things will change. Strangers called Earth Men will appear among you. Their skins are light-colored, and their ways are powerful. They clip their hair short and speak no Indian tongue. Follow nothing these Earth Men do, but keep your own ways that I have taught you as long as you can.
>
> The buffalo will disappear, at last, another animal will take its place, a slick animal with a long tail and split hoofs, whose flesh you will learn to eat. But first there will be another animal which you must learn to use. It has a shaggy neck and a tail almost touching the ground. Its hoofs are round. This animal will carry you on his back and help you in many ways. Those far hills that seem only a blue vision in the distance take many days to reach now; but with this animal you can get there in a short time, so fear him not. Remember what I have said.
>
> The Earth Men are too strong and his food will be too sweet and after we taste that food we will want it and forget our own foods. Chokecherries and plums, and wild turnips, and our honey from the wild bees, that is our food. This other food is too sweet. We eat it and forget.
>
> I am sorry to say these things, but I have seen them, and you will find that they will come true.[12]

After Sweet Medicine spoke, his people remained very quiet. They thought of his words and did not believe him. Silently they arose and left him alone in his lodge. The next day, when they returned, Sweet Medicine was gone. The Tsis Tsis Tas never saw him again.

Yellow Wolf remembered these stories and could not help but think of the prophecies he had seen come true. Surely these white men were the Earth Men about which Sweet Medicine had spoken.

---

[12] *Cheyenne Memories*, pp. 40–41.

These were white men, who drank the water which burned their throats and raped the land with wagons, buildings and other desecrations they brought from the lands of the east. These were the white men who called the Tsis Tsis Tas, "savages." Savages? Maybe, but the savagery of which the Tsis Tsis Tas were guilty lay in their belief in honesty, bravery and the chastity of their women.

These men were much different from Old Yellow Wolf's longtime friends, "White Hat" and "Little White Man." His two old friends understood the Tsis Tsis Tas ways, so much in fact that Little White Man married into the tribe. This happened when Old Yellow Wolf was no longer a young man, but not yet old. It happened when the land was still as Heammawihio had made it and the only white men around were an insignificant number of Spaniards and the fewer "hair faces" who traded and lived in the lands of the Tsis Tsis Tas and Arapaho. Their days on the plains would soon be gone and so too would be the Tsis Tsis Tas.

Yes, on the last day of his life, in the "Month of the Freezing Moon" (November) no one knows what Old Yellow Wolf's thoughts or feelings may have been. One thing was certain though, his people, the Tsis Tsis Tas, would lose their name and land. And on the twenty-ninth day of November, 1864, many would lose their lives. And for that brief instant before he breathed his last breath, Old Yellow Wolf may have wondered why Heammawihio stopped smiling on his people and why the unbroken stillness of the land would forever be haunted by autumn's song of sorrow.

2
The Brothers Bent

His years were ten and four they say
When he left St. Louis town,
He and brother Charles went west that day
And to Purgatory they were bound.

The Spaniards called it "El Rio de Las Animas Perdidas en Purgatorio," the River of Lost Souls in Purgatory, and yet this place was not the picture of gloom and despair as its name implied. Elk foraged in thickets of huge sunflowers, and wild turkeys, black bears and deer competed for succulent wild plums and cherries. In this land, blackbirds on cattails filled the air with their calls, while giant cottonwoods, gnarled with age, lined either side of a river whose slow surging waters gave life to the prairie itself. In its beauty, this rich bottomland offered refuge from the scorching heat of summer.

When summer turned to autumn, and wildflowers blossomed in profusion, giant grizzly bears arrived to hunt buffalo, their savage power something to behold. These 1200 pound bruins could chase down a young buffalo with bursts of speed up to thirty-five miles per hour. And yet, in their more docile and lethargic moments, they feasted on chokecherries and other delicacies before retiring to a winter's sleep. This land of plenty was also home to cougars, wolves, prairie chickens and great herds of antelope. However, there was more here than merely a gathering of the food chain. This land functioned as a natural oasis and as a wind break against the harshness of winter's snows.

Yellow Wolf and the other Cheyenne knew the mouth of the Purgatory River well. Legends of tragedy and death dwelled there, where the Cheyenne and Spanish alike related a story about this river's mouth. Before the Cheyenne owned horses, a group of Conquistadors ventured out to suppress all the Indians beyond the borders of Spain's new empire. And yet the sight of these curious men with "iron bellies,"[13] on magnificent four legged beasts, intrigued the Indians. When the Tsis Tsis Tas and other tribes first observed these men on animals, they thought they were monsters with two heads, four legs and a tail. But as the Indians approached the Conquistadors for a closer look, they discovered what glorious animals these strange men possessed. Some of the Tsis Tsis Tas said these men and animals were the ones mentioned in Sweet Medicine's prediction. Indian curiosity and Conquistador arrogance proved to be the catalysts that forever changed the course of Western history.

Once these Spaniards succeeded in their mission, the leaders disobeyed their orders to return to Mexico and chose instead to explore new lands. The age old struggle for supreme glory, however, erupted between the two leaders of the expedition. During an argument one night, they fought a duel to the death. The priests, who were always present on those expeditions,[14] told the remainder of the troops to abandon their campaign, for they now believed it to be cursed by God. Undaunted by the priests' warning, and without their blessing, Spain's conquerors continued on into the Great Plains' unknown vastness. Undaunted by the increasing number of Indians they encountered along the way, the Spanish journeyed until they came to the mouth of a river.

On the evening of their arrival, they set up camp. Confident about their superiority over any Indians, the Spaniards posted no sentries. Surely, they felt, these "root grubbers" could do no harm. Had not Pizzarro with only a hundred and sixty men conquered the Incan army of eighty thousand men of Peru? And had they not heard of Cabeza de Vaca's[15] eight year, six thousand mile journey,

---

[13]Indian name for Spanish armor's chest plates. Many of the plains tribes found relics of this armor and converted it to their own use, hence the nickname for many warriors throughout history as "Iron Belly."

[14]The political struggles between the Spanish Empire and the Holy Roman Church guaranteed the presence of priests. Spain sought its riches and the Church its converts and its portion of any treasures found.

[15]Cabeza de Vaca's name translated into English means Head of a Cow. For more on his remarkable story see *The Diaries of Cabeza de Vaca,* published by University of New Mexico Press.

following Indian trails and living off the land? During his odyssey de Vaca himself wrote about how mild and friendly were the tribes he and his three companions encountered. It was not the last time underestimating these natives would end in disaster. While those from Spain slept, Indians crept into their camp and started a grass fire. In the confusion, the Indians stole the horses and killed all the "iron bellies." Exceptions were a mulatto slave girl and a lone conquistador. Because he fought with such ferocity, the Indians spared his life. His knowledge of the horse, they knew, would be invaluable. Legends from both races told of this conquistador's elevation to a great chief of their tribe.

The Indians spoke of this battle as the time in "which we got horses."[16] The Spanish, however, spoke of men who died at the mouth of that river. According to the Hispanic tale, their souls were doomed forever, for they died without receiving the last rites of the Catholic Church. Since those days long ago, legends about these lost souls in purgatory have dwelled upon the banks of the river now called "Purgatory."

Yellow Wolf and his people frequently camped on the banks of another river, the Arkansas, some fifteen miles north of the Purgatory. As fertile as the "River of Lost Souls," no ill-begotten legends lurked upon its shores between midnight and morning. Over the next thirty years, the mouth of the River of Lost Souls and the banks of the Arkansas silently witnessed the events that forever changed the fates of two cultures and the men who belonged to both. These events also affected the lives of men whose blood was half white and half Indian.

In Yellow Wolf's fifty-third year of life, as he and his Hevhai-tanio warriors made their first expedition into the Red River country, the waters of the Purgatory and Arkansas Rivers were still pristine. On their way back north from stealing Comanche horses, near present day Pueblo, Colorado, they came across a stockade, on the Fountain River. Curious, they stopped to explore the origin of men who built this strange lodge of trees. Even more curious, the men within the stockade's confines could actually communicate with Yellow Wolf through Indian sign language. Yellow Wolf heard one man call himself Charles Bent and, though not a big man, he was slightly taller and stockier than the Cheyenne chief. But what

---

[16]Time frames for many of the plains tribes begin with, "In the time before we had horses" or "in the time after we had horses." The horse as a prized possession is akin to invention and evolution of the automobile in our society.

fascinated Yellow Wolf most about Bent was his white hat. Thereafter, Yellow Wolf called Charles Bent "White Hat."

Accompanying White Hat in 1827 was his seventeen-year-old brother, William. Yellow Wolf felt there was something different about these white men. They did not treat his people disrespectfully like the Spanish did. The Cheyenne chief particularly admired young William. He seemed to possess courage and understanding. Yellow Wolf thought he would have made a good Cheyenne, so in the custom of his people, he gave William a special name, "Skay-ah-veho—Little White Man."[17]

When the Bent brothers arrived in this area from St. Louis, the Fountain River was more of a creek than a river compared to the mighty Mississippi. Impractical for travel, the river was a great source of water for themselves, their stock and horses. The lack of trees and vegetation made this land seem more like a desert to the Bent brothers, who had known the lush green valleys of the Mississippi almost all of their lives.

Growing up in St. Louis, the gateway to the west, during the early nineteenth century was an adventure in itself for young William. Overlooking the Mississippi, elegant French houses with rich, green manicured lawns and fruit trees, aristocratically gazed down upon the streets of a bustling village. Those streets beckoned to young William, as they had his older brother Charles years before. Adventurers of all types packed old St. Louis' pathways. They enticed river men from keelboats, trappers with their freshly tanned wares and back woodsmen clad in old, smelly buckskin, who carried long rifles in their arms. The walkways were filled with Indians and slaves as well as black-robed priests and Sisters of Charity who shared the shade of locust trees lining the cobblestone streets. There were, of course, the ever present ladies of the night, who strolled the roadways after their midday awakening, as well as peasant women, brightly adorned in colored clothes, and sombreroed Mexican men. They were all part of this multi-ethnic citizenry. New England businessmen and government officials, one of whom was William's father, Silas Bent from the United States, were also present. St. Louis' streets abounded with adventure and excitement, for only eight and a half years before, Lewis and Clark had returned from the shores of the Pacific Ocean. While new

---

[17]Interview with Lucille Bent. (Lucille Bent and Ann Strange Owl have been very helpful in teaching the author what he knows of the Cheyenne language.)

expeditions departed almost daily to find an easy northwest passage, the streets continued to be filled with the sight and smell of furs. Fortunes amassed by their bloody harvests awaited those brave enough to venture into the uncharted regions of North America.

The paths of men searching for adventure often crossed here, but more common, their journey began in this city with the simple cry of a newborn baby. William Wells Bent was born to Silas and Martha Bent on May 23, 1809, the sixth of their eleven children. After fourteen years, the vibrance of the streets and call to adventure would lure him away to the land of the Cheyenne. For William, Lewis and Clark's expedition, three years before his birth, profoundly effected his life as well as those of thousands of people who followed him west .

When William was seven years old, his brother Charles journeyed from St. Louis to begin a fur trading venture. In 1816, he traveled to Lakota land on the upper Missouri River. At five-feet seven inches, Charles was not a big man, but he possessed a tenacious will to succeed. The violent trade wars created by the lucrative fur business caused Charles and a Frenchman named Ceran St. Vrain to seek new avenues of opportunity. They found them in Mexico. They journeyed west to an adobe village called Taos. Seeking to exploit this village and the town of Santa Fe, Bent and St. Vrain courted Mexico's most affluent business leaders. Bent and St. Vrain knew cooperation with these men could fulfill a dream that had existed for years. The vision was an overland trading route called the Santa Fe Trail. The existence of this trail allowed the two young adventurers to set up a partnership around 1827. Seventeen-year-old William joined them later in the year.

On the banks of the Fountain River, in present day South-central Colorado, the Brothers Bent and St. Vrain decided to build a stockade. Here, they reasoned, was a pivotal location for fur trappers and mountain men to rest and trade their wares and not worry about going to larger trading posts hundreds of miles away. Their stockade flourished for a couple of years, but then one day, something unexpected happened — a chance meeting with other curious newcomers to the area — the Cheyenne.

The Bents realized Yellow Wolf was intrigued by them and they talked for hours in sign language about what the Bents were doing this far west. Surely, the Cheyenne chief told them, they must know the buffalo never came this far west in the winter time; and where the buffalo roamed, so did his people. Though the Bents and St.

Vrain constructed their stockade to trade with white men, Yellow Wolf told them of a more fertile river area 60 miles east. The visionary Cheyenne chief, advised his new friends to build a new fort in the land they called "Big Timbers." He told them if they moved there, he would not only bring in his clan, but other Cheyenne and Arapaho clans as well. He felt both races could benefit each other by this trade alliance.

This idea had never entered Charles Bent's mind before. After some serious thought about its consequences and long discussion with his favorite brother, Charles considered Yellow Wolf's proposal. The Bents agreed to move their post to the Big Timbers, and in 1831 Charles Bent and company began building an adobe fort, the very first in Colorado. The Bents hired one hundred Mexican peons from Taos to build their fort, not for military personnel, but for trading purposes. They completed it between 1835 and 1836. Ironically, the fort's site was much closer to the Santa Fe Trail than their original stockade. Soon people from every walk of life — trappers, traders, hunters, freighters — traveled there. In time, some brought their wives and children.

The fort was built as a hollow rectangle 150 feet by 100 feet with a dirt floor and six-foot-thick adobe walls, impervious to fire. There were twenty-five rooms throughout the compound. Periodically, who ever occupied the room would sprinkle the dirt floor with water to keep down the dust. At the center of the fort's courtyard was a well, and ice was available from the ice house. When Samuel and Susan Magoffin arrived at Bent's Fort on their way along the Santa Fe Trail,[18] she described its sight in her diary, "Well, the outside exactly fills my idea of an ancient castle. It is built of adobe, unburnt brick, and Mexican style so far. The walls are very high and very thick with rounding corners. There is but one entrance, this is to the East rather."[19] All of the rooms had wooden doors with metal hasps and latches. In the autumn and winter months, fireplaces burned almost constantly in all of the sleeping quarters, even though the fort's thick adobe walls kept out the cold winds. Those who stayed at the fort saw every kind of man, woman and beast. In the evenings the Magoffins and others treated themselves to the music of guitars and voices of the Mexican laborers

---

[18]Samuel Magoffin was a very wealthy man. Before he and his young wife Susan departed on their journey, he purchased a milk cow and laying hens for her eating and drinking pleasures. This luxury was unheard of by most of the Trail's travelers.

[19]*Down the Santa Fe Trail and Into Mexico — Diaries of Susan Shelby Magoffin.* p. 60.

and vaqueros which swept through the fort. The music sometimes soothed the pregnant, nineteen-year-old Susan. She cherished those times, but fighting, initiated by the drinking and gambling amongst the trappers and hunters often drowned out her musical pleasures. The presence of a "billiards room" shocked the very proper Susan Magoffin. The constant quarrelling among the Mexican women working for the Bents disturbed her and became yet another "common" occurrence from which Susan's wealthy upbringing had, until that time, sheltered her. In the daytime, Susan heard the constant pounding of hammers, as the fort's blacksmith and livestock handlers kept busy outside of her room. She often awoke to the sounds of children playing or crying outside. One morning, braying donkeys and mules awakened her. Susan struggled with her health during her stay and within a few days of her arrival, she miscarried her child. Susan Magoffin was probably the first white woman who braved the Santa Fe Trail in the later stages of pregnancy. She buried her child at Bent's Fort.

Along with many others, the Cheyenne regularly visited Bent's Fort. When times were bad, they relied on "Little White Man" to help. Indians, never allowed to stay in the fort over night, were permitted to camp outside its gates. But during daylight hours, they filled the fort with their presence and trade goods. Many white visitors feared these people they did not comprehend, while others held nothing but disdain for these painted "savages." To them, the Cheyenne were lazy, worthless and no good thieves. "Skay-ah-veho — Little White Man" knew better.

Reconstruction of Bent's old Fort on its original site 8 miles outside of La Junta, Colorado.

Upon his fort's completion, Bent pursued his trading and his friendship with the Cheyenne. With each passing day he spent with them, William's fondness for Yellow Wolf and his people grew. He found they possessed many qualities most whites did not. The Cheyenne were truthful in a paradoxical way. If they stole a horse, they admitted the theft to their victim when asked. Their word was their bond. The Cheyenne upheld honesty and looked down on no one, for the tribe as a whole meant life. Every man, woman and child, whether religious zealots, contraries or homosexuals were all accepted members of the tribe. Their sense of justice and humor and their vitality made them special to young William.

Their eating habits awed any white witnessing it for the first time. Yellow Wolf and other Cheyenne men astonished William with the amount of food they consumed at a single sitting. Bent once observed Yellow Wolf eat ten pounds of buffalo meat and still crave more. Yet this chief of the Hevhaitanio clan stood only five-feet-six inches tall and weighed 125 pounds. As William learned from his more frequent contacts with the Cheyenne and other plains tribes, this type of gluttony was not uncommon. Within time, Little White Man learned the Cheyenne language, customs and deities and yet he longed to know more about these people he called friend. As time passed, William found himself more like the Cheyenne around him than he was like a white Missourian.

During this same time, Little White Man saw her. He instinctively knew Owl Woman, still only a child, was special. She walked with an air of confidence among her own very proud people. As William Bent's years with Owl Woman's people passed, her beauty matured from a young girl to a woman. The sight of her did things to his insides William didn't quite understand. After all, he wasn't a boy any longer. At twenty-eight, Skay-Ah-Veho had not yet experienced courtship's rituals. He knew his pain wasn't just from the loneliness of this country, because many whites now stayed at the fort on a regular basis, and while in Taos, he experienced the night-time pleasures of the town's senoritas. Yet this Cheyenne woman's beauty stirred up more than just a burning desire in him. (What young man hadn't experienced lust before?) William wanted Owl Woman for his wife.

Owl Woman and her younger sister, Yellow Woman, were the daughters of White Thunder, Keeper of the Sacred Medicine Arrows. In the Cheyenne hierarchy, this Keeper of the Sacred Medicine Arrows represented unity for their nations. So in 1837,

William "Skay Ah Veho" (Little White Man) Bent.   Photo courtesy Colorado Historic Society

Little White Man rode alone out into the wintery plains of Southern Colorado to find a certain Cheyenne village to meet White Thunder. He brought many horses packed with gifts. And when he arrived at the village, he found no problem locating his lodge. As if drawn by a magnet, William passed the many brightly painted lodges and the friendly faces of the people he had grown to love until he stopped his horse in front of White Thunder's lodge.

The horses and gifts they bore were for White Thunder. If the gifts were accepted, Little White Man would be permitted to court Owl Woman. Fortunately for Bent, his bargaining skills and diplomacy remained important in this situation. After what seemed an eternity, the Keeper of the Medicine Arrows at last accepted his gifts. As he did, he smiled, for he liked Skay-Ah-Veho. Village voices and drums filled the night with music and song as a the ritual courting of Owl Woman, the daughter of the Keeper of the Sacred Medicine Arrows, had begun — Cheyenne style. William remembered this sacred engagement period during which they made him stay alone in a lodge. He recalled how Owl Woman, clothed in her finest beaded buckskin dress, brought him food and drink each day. William vividly remembered the sight of her body and her sound as she moved about the lodge with her beaded moccasined feet. He also recalled the sight of Owl Woman's favorite shell earrings peeking out beneath her raven colored hair, which she parted down the middle of her head. In Cheyenne custom, her braided hair was tied with strips of buckskin and William recalled how vermilion shone upon her cheeks like the blush of a rose. Dressed this way, she delivered a promise of fulfillment. Her perfumed fragrance of sweet grass and sage filled his sense and she smelled of her daily baths in the waters of rivers and streams.[20] She was Little White Man's promise of life, as the waters of the plains were life to the Cheyenne.

Little White Man longed to be alone with Owl Woman, but Cheyenne custom forbade him. The courting ritual required her to be accompanied by a young girlfriend or sister. As the only ceremony, on their wedding night, Little White Man's friends carried Owl Woman to his lodge. She was dressed in the clothing he brought her, and his other gifts covered her arms and neck. Owl Woman also brought her protective rope. Again Cheyenne custom

---

[20]Unlike the women of his own race, in the early nineteenth century, Cheyenne women bathed every day in all seasons. If the weather was too severe, they bathed in their lodges.

caused more frustration for William. The bride wore a protective rope for the first few nights of their marriage. This braided cord circled her waist beneath her clothing, winding around her thighs down to her knees. It was worn so the husband and wife could truly learn to see each other without being blinded by their passions. William respected the rope. Once removed, it meant he was welcome and Little White Man became married to a woman of his adopted Cheyenne.

In January, 1838, ten months after their marriage, Owl Woman gave birth to her first child, a girl named after William's sister, Mary. It was a time for celebration, not only for the birth, but for the Bent brothers and Ceran St. Vrain. The business they started from nothing boomed on the frontier. The fort began seeing the likes of Kit Carson, Jim Beckwourth, "Crazy" Bill Williams, Jim Bridger, John C. Fremont, and other men who became legends in their own time. All of these men ventured west and crossed the River of Lost Souls in search of what was over the next hill and valley. And below and beyond those places, they found Bent's Fort.

From 1836 to 1838, William managed the company's fort. His brother Charles had moved to Taos. The older Bent still worked for the company, but his primary task centered on building up trade and surveying land for the Mexican government. There, he settled down and married Maria Ignacia Jaramillo, a beautiful Mexican widow.

1839 and 1840 proved fruitful for the Bents, in both trade and family. Owl Woman gave birth, this time to a son, whom William named Robert, in honor of his brother who had worked at the fort since 1836. William remembered these years with pride because everything in life he held precious seemed to be his. Even overwhelmed with his business success, his love for Owl Woman never diminished. She and their children were the source of his greatest pride. This daughter of White Thunder enhanced his life and enriched his soul as each season became a fleeting memory of the moments they shared in love. He sometimes despised his obligations at the fort, for they kept him away from Owl Woman and her people. Their customs and values became what he most cherished in mankind. His thoughts however, returned to reality and William put forth all of his efforts to make all trading post visitors welcome.

Indians who frequented Bent's Fort included Moke-Tavato — Black Kettle, White Antelope and the Arapaho chiefs, Neva and Left Hand. In return, Skay-Ah-Veho's children, Mary and Robert accompanied their mother to her village. William wanted his children educated in both cultures. He knew in order to survive in the ever changing west, his children must learn Cheyenne honesty and understand the treachery and greed of some whites. He felt his children must know that evil existed where good prevailed in life.

For years, wagon trains filled with traders, trappers and adventures of all types travelled in and out of Bent's Fort. One of the Bent brothers sometimes led these trains because they knew the country and were well known to the Cheyenne and Arapaho. Although they lived in peace with the whites, Cheyenne enemies often invaded their lands. In autumn of 1841, the first of the Bent brothers died. In October, Robert left the wagon train he led to hunt buffalo. A couple of miles beyond the caravan's safety, marauding Comanches attacked, killed and scalped him. His brothers, William, Charles and George, were devastated by the loss of their youngest sibling. The tragedy left them with the realization, death is a common visitor to all, and when a loved one is murdered, it becomes more intimate and obscene.

Summer of 1843 held two surprises for William Bent. His third child and second son was born to Owl Woman. They named him George, in honor of William's brother. Secondly, like a gust of west wind, his old friend Kit Carson suddenly appeared at Bent's Fort. A beautiful Mexican girl accompanied him from New Mexico. Named Josefa Jaramillo, she was the sister of Charles' wife, Maria Ignacia. A few nights later, after a big fandango,[21] Josefa and Carson married, making Kit Carson a brother-in-law to the brothers Bent.[22]

Three years later, life changed for both the Bents and the Cheyenne. On a warm May day, in a city 2,000 miles east of their land, a group of men declared war on another country. Their action set into motion a mass migration that forever changed the face of the west. In early summer of 1846, Moke-Tavato or Black Kettle began hearing incredible stories from other warriors. He listened as they described the vast numbers of white warriors sighted, riding horseback towards Little White Man's fort. They told Black Kettle they carried long knives and dressed in blue coat uniforms. The most unbelievable tale of all spoke of the sheer number of soldiers his warriors counted — 1,700! Black Kettle did not believe this many white people existed, let alone white warriors!

---

[21]A "fandango" is a big dance, a celebration.
[22]Some reports state that Carson and Josefa had already been married in Taos, N.M.

The chiefs of the Cheyenne clans gathered and rode to Little White Man's fort to see this sight. Even as they observed this vast army of warriors, it continued to be very difficult for the Cheyenne to fully understand the magnitude of what they witnessed. Incredulously, they watched as Little White Man welcomed this army of whites. Bent later told Black Kettle war had broken out between his country and the land where his brother, Charles "White Hat," lived. Black Kettle further learned this army, considered small by white men, was riding on horseback to invade Mexico's territories under the command of Stephen Watts Kearny. Black Kettle never forgot this sight, for if this were a small army, what would a large army look like? His thoughts made him feel insignificant and he was frightened for his people.

The crisis passed with the troop's departure, but the following year brought great sorrow to Little White Man's world. It began with Charles' death. During the previous August, William had heard of General Kearny's successful conquest of Mexico. Without firing a shot he put down the rebellion in what is now New Mexico. Soon after, Kearny appointed Charles Territorial Governor. According to Kit Carson's account to William, Pueblo Indians had revolted one cold January morning, in Taos, while Charles visited there on business. As peacemaker, William's older brother attempted to calm the rebellious Pueblos. However, they were drunk from celebrating, having tasted blood earlier that day when they had murdered and cut to pieces any American they found. Charles' negotiations with them failed. He chose not to fight them, fearing his wife and other women present might be harmed. Bent lay down his arms and approached the Indians. Without hesitation they shot and stabbed him to death, leaving him horribly mutilated. The Indians then took his scalp and tacked the bloody piece on a board with brass nails. They sang, chanted and screamed as they paraded his scalp throughout the town.

When news of White Hat's death reached the Cheyenne, Yellow Wolf told Little White Man he would gather his warriors and journey to this place to avenge their old mentor's death. Touched by his offer, Skay-Ah-Veho thanked his friend, but informed him it wasn't necessary. He told Yellow Wolf the white man's army had put the rebellion down. Over 250 Pueblo Indians and Mexicans paid for Charles' death with their lives.

Seven months later, tragedy struck again. While giving birth to William's fourth child, whom he later named Julia, Owl Woman died.[23] In Cheyenne custom, her relatives dressed Owl Woman in all of her finery, then gently placed her body on a scaffold in the branches of a cottonwood tree. This way, the Wise One Above could easily find her. He would then be her guide across the four great rivers and would take her along the Milky Way's route to a place called Seyan. Little White Man arrived too late to share her last moments, but she left a legacy of four children and an aching void in his heart no other woman would ever again fill. Anyone who knew William Bent and Owl Woman said their love for each other never wavered. After her untimely death and up until his own, Little White Man never stopped missing or loving her. Her death signaled the start of two decades of sorrow for Little White Man and his beloved Cheyenne.

Within three months after Owl Woman's death, William's brother, George, died at the fort of a "wasting away" disease. Some said he died of consumption. A few months later, overwhelmed with grief and concern for his four motherless children, William, in Cheyenne custom, married Owl Woman's sister, Yellow Woman. His decision was easy. He needed someone to care for his children and Yellow Woman's face was familiar to her four nieces and nephews.

In 1849, Yellow Woman bore William Bent his fifth child, a third son. William named him Charles after his brother. This boy child, some say, was in fact the Devil incarnate. In fifteen years, the west fell prey to his wrath and hatred. However, before Charles became a year old, his father, William Wells Bent, destroyed the fort he, his brothers and Ceran St. Vrain carved out of the Great Plains' wilderness. With blasts of gun powder, he blew up his home and business of almost twenty years so it couldn't be used as a military fortification. Little White Man's world was changing far too quickly for him and the Cheyenne he loved. With his wife and five children he departed this land and traveled southeast to a new life awaiting him some thirty-eight miles away.

With the dawn's arrival, he left behind his home, his business, the bodies of his three brothers and his beloved wife, Owl Woman. But his heart remained in this land of the Tsis Tsis Tas, in this place not far from the River of Lost Souls — a place full of change and sorrow.

---

[23]There is controversy as to whether this child was Julia or Charles. Lucille Bent and some historians claim the child was Charles, but George Bent in his letters to George Hyde repeatedly refers to Charles as "my half-brother." "Life of George Bent," p. 83.

3
There's Gold In Colorado

In eighteen and fifty-eight,
Where the Cherry Creek joins the Platte,
They came in wagons by the droves,
'Cause Denver's where it's at.

Autumn of 1858 started out uneventful, but before the year ended, Little White Man wished he could turn back the hands of time. Changes in his world between the end of the Mexican War and his new fort's construction brought a deluge of nineteenth century pilgrims seeking their place in the newly conquered promised lands of "New" Mexico.

In this early autumn, William's business boomed in his new fort of stone. There, Indians and whites alike traded regularly with Bent and each other. His fort also became a regular wayfarer's stop for anyone traveling the Santa Fe Trail. For the "Trail" was now a common, but often deadly thoroughfare through these lands of the Cheyenne and Arapaho.

To the Cheyenne and other plains tribes, the flow of whites seemed endless. This period of transition found the Cheyenne and Arapaho in a strange predicament. They were now trapped between two great floods of whites. To the north lay the Oregon Trail and at the Arkansas River was the Santa Fe. Between these two great roads rested the very heart of the Cheyenne and Arapaho hunting grounds. Within a year, another trail diagonally cut across these two wagon roads. It followed the Platte River for two hundred miles from present day Julesburg, Colorado, to Denver. The thousands who traveled it named the trail after the river.

The immigrants' exodus from their eastern lands drastically changed the lives of the Cheyenne. However, other changes, even more noticeable to the Indians, were overtaking the land itself. The speed with which these interlopers made the huge groves of cotton-wood trees disappear astounded Black Kettle and the others. His people had made their winter camp there for years. Within a year, even the Big Timbers showed signs of vanishing. The whites cut the trees down, then used the timber for houses, wagons, towns and tool handles. The grass for miles around was eaten down to the ground by their cattle herds, causing the buffalo to migrate to other grasslands. Black Kettle knew the buffalo herds' decrease meant hunger for his people. This conflict of one race's greed for another's land was nothing new to mankind, but its causes perplexed Black Kettle. His people lived in harmony with the land and respected nature's ways. The white man though seemed bent on destroying the natural order of things to "civilize" his surroundings. Worse than the land's destruction, however, was the invisible death these white men brought with them — civilization's diseases.

Black Kettle vividly remembered the cholera epidemic these wandering white men carried with them in 1849. His people called it the "Cramps"[24] and hundreds of them died. Little White Man's son, George, recollected journeying to a Cheyenne village with his stepmother as a seven year old child to escape the cholera. He remembered his people's fear at this village and recalled a Cheyenne warrior who jumped on his horse with his weapons and chanted, "If I could see this thing, if I knew where it was, I would go there and kill it!"[25] The warrior then fell from his horse with the Cramps and died.

That same night burned vivid scars into George's young memory. In the flickering shadows of the firelit darkness, he saw his grandmother, White Thunder's widow, alive for the last time. His last moments with her changed him. He peered into her sunken eyes and remembered how they once sparkled at the sight of him.

[24] *Life of George Bent*, p. 96.
[25] *Life of George Bent*, p. 97.

He recalled, too, how her now gaunt and hollow face replaced the smile that once accentuated her high cheek bones. And the warmth of her loving embraces were now cold to touch as she felt clammy and fought to breath just one more breath. Then, it too stopped as she died.

At another village they journeyed to, the images of men, women and children laying dead in and around their lodges, wiped out by this unseen assassin were etched in George's memory. The filth of the white man's cities bred and nurtured this murderer cholera, a product of their unclean nineteenth century living conditions. They carried the shackles of this contagious disease in their wagons as they traveled across Cheyenne and Arapaho land. Like their diseases, which included measles, chicken pox, and a variety of venereal plights, the whites seemed to have no end.

Bull Bear, a leader of the Cheyenne Dog Soldier society,[26] observed the white man for years, but had never before witnessed such a wide variety of them. They arrived in every size, shape and age and began to saturate these lands with wagons and horses. He felt a blind warrior could follow the trail left by the debris fallen off their wagons or purposely discarded.

Bull Bear remembered these people's many hair colors — blond, black and red. Sometimes many of those combinations could be seen in one wagon. The strange skin markings further puzzled him, particularly those with red hair. They wore red dots all over their faces. Impishly, he considered taking some of those colorful scalp locks to decorate his lance. Other Cheyenne though, turned their thoughts to eastern lands. Surely with all of the whites coming west, there must be vacant land from whence they came!

However, other observers of this pilgrimage became angry. Warrior societies of Cheyenne, Arapaho, Kiowa, Pawnee and Comanche tribes frequently raided the whites. In return, white men shot at any Indian man, woman or child they confronted on the trail, just for the sport of it. As a result of these interactions, tensions grew and both races blamed each other for the hunger they suffered.

Five years earlier, in 1853, nine year old George Bent and his siblings were sent to Westport, Missouri.[27] Their father owned a large farm there and he wanted his children educated in white

---

[26]The Cheyenne had many societies, among them were the fierce warriors of the Dog Soldiers.
[27]Present day Kansas City, Missouri.

schools. Ten years passed before he and his brother Charles gazed upon their mother's people again. William left his children in Albert D. Boone's care, a grandson of Daniel Boone and close personal friend of Bent. With his new fort completed, William continued his lucrative trading business with the Cheyenne and other tribes on the Upper Arkansas. In addition, the U. S. Government contracted with him to haul their freight throughout the region. Bent sent parties out from his fort to trade regularly with the masses of people traveling the Oregon and Santa Fe trails. But every spring, Little White Man himself hauled a load of goods to Westport, Missouri. He wanted time with his children.

No matter where he traveled, Skay-Ah-Veho saw his adopted people were troubled. White settlers were also vexed. Tensions caused by the differences of two cultures vying for the same land brought an outcry from the settlers for protection. The U.S. Government must defend them against the "savages" who roamed the plains. The cry was answered and soon the ominous presence of "blue coat" soldiers became more and more prevalent in the land of the Cheyenne and Arapaho.

In May and June of 1858, the "time when the horses get fat,"[28] an accelerator for the eventual decimation of the Cheyenne and Arapaho people was discovered where the Cherry Creek joins the Platte River — gold! Near a tiny settlement called Auraria, a man named William Green Russell found some gold dust. It wasn't much, and when he searched for more, little could be found. Rumors spread like cholera to the scattered cabins and town sites congregated between those two bodies of water and almost immediately hundreds of people arrived to hunt for the most precious of white man's metals.

To Neva and his Arapaho, camped peaceably nearby, it became quite a sight. He could not understand what was happening. What would make any man do these things? The Arapaho chief watched in amazement as white men stole and sold town sites from each other on land belonging to his people, even people whom Neva knew acted strangely, like "Old" John Smith. Years before this mountain man and trader had married an Arapaho woman. He successfully convinced many new arrivals his wife owned the land he sold.

---

[28]Cheyenne describe the months of the year in accordance with nature's effects on the land and animals.

One township site called St. Charles was stolen from a miner named Charley Nichols. Nine men on horseback forced him off the land on which he built his cabin. Not eager to fight nine armed men, Nichols decided to do battle in court. Fighting for the legal ownership of his claim lasted almost a year, but when the courts settled the litigation in Charley's favor, it was too late. Possession remained in the claim jumpers' hands. One of the nine claim jumpers, the newly appointed Sheriff of Arapaho County, Edward Wynkoop renamed this stolen claim "Denver," in honor of James W. Denver, the Territorial Governor of Kansas. By the time Charley returned, much of early Denver had already been built. By then, the real gold rush was on!

To the Cheyenne, these "Pike's Peakers" were a strange breed of men indeed. They traveled across the prairies in search of yellow gold on horseback, in wagons and on foot. There were young, old and even feeble. Sometimes the Cheyenne found stragglers lost in the prairie, half out of their minds for want of food and water. On more than one occasion, these dazed, gold seeking pilgrims awoke to find themselves in an Indian village, nursed back to health. The Cheyenne felt these white men truly crazy to do all they did for this yellow metal. After all, their cousins, the Arapaho, had made bullets from this soft metal for years.[29]

In 1859, 140,000 gold seekers ventured west to Colorado, discovering only two big strikes, one in Central City and the other in Idaho Springs. The same year, the City of Denver became chartered, the Rocky Mountain News issued its first edition, and Little White Man sold his second fort to the War Department (now called the Department of Defense). Shortly after the sale of his fort, the government appointed Little White Man Indian Agent for the Cheyenne and other tribes with whom he lived and traded for over twenty years.

William "Skay-Ah-Veho," Bent did not want the job of Indian Agent, but War Department purchased his fort for a military post. To ensure the Indians received their annuities on time and in good condition he took the job. Two years before, the government engaged in treaty talks with the Cheyenne and Arapaho. It was the first time they had tasted the bitter lies brought by eastern Indian agents. Lies gave birth to hunger and hunger begat the anger

---

[29]This is a traditional Arapaho tale that was shared by Paul Hanway (an Arapaho Vietnam Veteran).

which often turned to violence. Because of this and the ever increasing "white tide," William didn't want to see any hostilities breaking out. It was obvious by then, the Indians didn't trust the government, but they did trust Little White Man.

The following year, a miner named Abe Lee unearthed a huge gold strike near Leadville, so big in fact, he reportedly exclaimed, when he discovered it, "Lord A'Mighty! I've got all Californy in my pan!" By then, the news reached back east telling of the abundant wealth to be found in the Kansas Territory.

In the interim, the Cheyenne and other plains Indians continued to be pushed off their lands. Angered by it, their isolated raids on these white intruders became more frequent. Tens of thousands of white people now ventured west to Colorado. This surging tide of seemingly endless immigrants was not a new sight for Little White Man. He beheld these same kinds of adventurers as a boy in St. Louis, except then, they sought fur trading routes. Denver's streets, like those of St. Louis, soon filled with all kinds of people. Buffalo hunters could be smelled, down wind, from two blocks away, and gambling houses, saloons and the ever-present ladies of the night lined the dust- and mud-covered streets. Like shepherds armed with a deck of cards, dandified gamblers took their trade to saloons to fleece the newly arrived sheep of their cash. Miners, settlers and gunmen, Southerners and Northerners alike, drifted into these rough and tumble towns. Panhandlers, too, arrived looking for a "grubstake," as well as medicine show barkers, who appeared in colorful wagons amidst the hooplah of their sideshows. Also present were the curious Cheyenne and Arapaho. They watched as one of their favorite campsites vanished under the cover of these assorted whites. However, their curiosity turned to outrage on an April night in 1860.

At the invitation of mountain man Jim Beckwourth, a band of Cheyenne and Apache arrived in Denver to trade their buffalo robes. On the evening of their visit, a group of drunken "bummers"[30] stumbled into the Indian lodges and raped and beat both their old and young women. Three stolen Indian mules were later recovered by Cheyenne warriors, who tracked them down some ten miles off.

In a letter to the *Rocky Mountain News,* dated April 18, 1860, Beckwourth deplored these acts of violence against the Cheyenne and Apache visitors and stated,

---

[30]A western term for a person or persons too lazy to work, but not too lazy to steal.

Where the Cherry Creek joins the South Platte River, about 1859.

Denver, about 1859.

Photo courtesy Colorado Historic Society

The Indians are as keenly sensible to acts of injustice, as they are tenacious of revenge, and it is more humiliating to them to be recipients of such treatment upon their own lands, which they have been deprived of, their game driven off and they made to suffer by hunger, and when they pay us a visit, abused more than dogs . . . All of our Indian troubles are produced by imprudent acts of unprincipled white men.

Beckwourth's words remained unheeded in those turbulent times. The law was slow in coming west. Division in American unity easily found its way to almost every corner of this muddy way station, located where the Cherry Creek joined the Platte River. Many of these "bummers" and immigrants were staunch Unionists, but others followed the South's belief in secession and the right to own slaves. They voiced their opinions in streets or crowded saloons in the new city of Denver. Sometimes, this led to fist fights and brawls, but more often someone lay shot or stabbed.

The metamorphosis of prairie land into boom town irrevocably transformed the west, as the United States prepared to divide itself on the bloody battlefields of civil war. Some of the explosive fragments of this division found its way to the Colorado and New Mexico Rockies. Yes, the law of man was slow in coming to Denver, but the word of God quickly reached this city in 1859 and 1860.

Episcopal Reverend John H. Kehler first held church services in the Criterion Saloon on Larimer Street because no church existed. When he initially arrived in Denver, he duly noted the extreme difficulties of holding services in this den of iniquity. As one parishioner recalled on that first Sunday,

> the gambling was carried on the first floor while the preaching was proceeding on the second. The flooring was rough boards with wide cracks between them and every word uttered by the occupants of the saloon, including those at the gaming tables, was as plainly heard by the congregation as the sermon.[31]

But, Reverend Kehler's parish records his congregation's greatest trials were several untimely deaths. Of the first twelve funeral services he performed, five men were murdered and two others hanged for murder. There was one suicide and one death due to alcoholism.[32] Causes of death for the other three were not recorded. Times proved challenging for a timid man of God.

---

[31] *The City and the Saloon — Denver 1858–1916*, p. 13.
[32] Ibid.

However, that, too, changed in the City of Denver. On May 4, 1860, a giant of a man rode into town, the new Methodist preacher. He had recently arrived from the frontier hamlets of Nebraska to bring his word of God to the ungodly and he preached his sermons from the holy scriptures or from the truths according to his huge fists! His name was John Milton Chivington.

4
The Gun Toting Parson

Like a devil born from Hell,
In the morning light he came,
And history still retells
That Chivington was his name.

At six-feet-four and a half inches tall with 260 pounds of solid muscle, he was easily a man folks looked up to. His bull neck, massive barrel chest and thick arms accrued an unbelievable strength from an early life of hard work in the timber business. His reddish-brown hair set off his piercing black eyes — eyes some men said looked right through their very souls. His imposing frame looked even larger when one added two forty-four Colt revolvers to his hips and placed him behind the pulpit of Denver's Methodist Church. The Reverend John Milton Chivington's rich baritone voice reverberated throughout the saloon walls in which he first preached. Later the foundations of his small log church on Larimer Street seemed to tremble from the force of his sermons. If necessary he could preach hot hell or hot lead and according to those who knew him, he feared neither man nor beast.

John M. Chivington arrived in Denver in 1860, when the "Queen City of the West" was just a fledgling frontier hamlet. Hearing news of gold strikes in Colorado, Chivington decided to set up his house of God in this hell-raising way station to the mountains.

Some folks called Chivington the "fighting parson," a nickname he earned during his early preaching days in the Kansas-Missouri borders. Those same folks said the Reverend inherited his father Isaac's size, strength and fighting temperament. At age thirty-nine, this wasn't his first frontier church, but this temple of God became his last. Because of his love for a good fight and the outbreak of the Civil War, John Chivington changed from a man of God to a warrior. And life cast him into a paradoxical controversy that to this day, still pervades the very mention of his name!

Some say history and hatred led Chivington to this controversy. Others declare, "Sister Fate" charted his life before his birth. And the charted course began in 1790, when John Chivington's father, Isaac, came into the world. While this infant cried, ten year old Yellow Wolf listened to the old men's tales of their origin. In the Cheyenne chief's third decade of life, young Isaac settled in Warren County, Ohio's wilderness, with his bride, Jane Runyon. Isaac soon put his six-feet six-inch two hundred and fifty pound frame to task by clearing the two sections of heavily wooded land he purchased, unaware that over a thousand miles west of his home, a five-foot six-inch Cheyenne counted coup on his enemies and stole their horses.

Though their coup yelps were not audible in Ohio's wilderness in 1812, Isaac did hear war's distant sounds as he marched off to fight in Canada. He served under General William Henry Harrison, who defeated British and Indian forces poised against him at the Thames River. Among his enemy casualties was the great Shawnee chief Tecumseh. In America's second war, Isaac learned the art of battle, while in Colorado's plains, a chief named Yellow Wolf taught young braves the art of Cheyenne warfare. The paths of these two men never crossed. But their actions in those years influenced the life of Isaac's son, John.

Born in Ohio's harsh frontier wilderness on January 27, 1821, John Milton Chivington came into the world without a whimper. He grew up and helped tame the forested valleys of Warren County. His father chose farming as a career, but because of the terrain, his vocation proved to be impractical to support his young family. In order to make any profit, Isaac cleared his land of trees and brush. From this timber he sold hardwood lumber to the area's new settlers. Isaac learned they were anxious to buy the fruits of his hard labor so they could build their homes and barns. He realized these trees provided a good income, and in order to increase his cash flow, young Chivington traded his lumber with Cincinnati merchants twenty miles away. As his business flourished, so did his family, and within a single decade's span, his wife Jane gave birth to six children. Only four, though, survived into adulthood, three boys and a girl.

The Chivington brothers, John, Lewis and Isaac, Jr. matured to great size and strength, while their sister Sarah resembled her mother in size and features. Life was hard, yet good for these children on the Ohio frontier. John's earliest memories of this period were vague shadows of his mother, who aged before her time. In 1826, when John reached his fifth year, tragedy befell the Chivington family. Though history didn't record the cause of Isaac's death at age thirty-six, the responsibility of raising four fatherless children fell on Jane Chivington's shoulders. At fifteen, Lewis, John's oldest brother, managed the family's timber business, while the younger children helped their mother cultivate the cleared land.

In the evenings, Jane educated her children, for there were no established schools in the area. Southwestern Ohio did have an occasional circuit teacher, who journeyed there for short periods of time. However, for the most part, John and Sarah completed their primary education at home through their mother's tutoring from what few books existed in their family library. John's thirst for knowledge was insatiable. On one of the family trips to Cincinnati, his mother purchased a dictionary. From this book, Milton's *Paradise Lost*, a Bible, and a worn, leather Episcopalian prayer book, young John acquired a vast vocabulary. He lost himself for hours in this fascinating world of words when time permitted.

From the Bible, his imagination soared at the tales of Samson smiting Philistines with his massive strength or Daniel's total devotion to God while he awaited a deadly fate in the lion's den. From the pages of Milton, young John tingled while he read of the Devil's gathering legions readying to battle the Hosts of Heaven. What boy or man wouldn't be fascinated by those times when God's forces waged battle against evil itself? Sometimes, when he let his mind wander, he tried to imagine what a remarkable spectacle that battle would have been. John must have held fond memories of those special times, but sadly, his education halted when he reached thirteen. He was maturing now in character and physical strength, and his family needed John in their timber business. Young

Chivington never lost his love of the written and spoken word. In his later life, he was both articulate and eloquent.

A perfectionist, John Chivington showed his skills in lumbering, for all of his wood cuts were precise and hewn as smoothly as if they had been planed. As he finished each cut, John carefully branded his initials on each end of the wood. His meticulous attention to detail eventually led his family to promote him.

At age eighteen, Chivington took over marketing the family business. Consequently, he spent more and more time in the city of Cincinnati. On one of these trips, John first gazed upon Martha Rollason while she worked in a friend's household. She wasn't beautiful, but there was something about this girl that caught John's inquisitive eye and heart. Maybe she excited his interest with her soft Virginian accent or by the fact she held her own in intelligent conversations. Behind her round brown eyes, she possessed a mind educationally superior to John's. Martha could read and write in both French and English. Although short in stature, she never avoided hard physical labor when called upon. Martha displayed mannerisms and education uncommon to a household servant. During the course of Chivington's short courtship of Martha, she divulged she had been highly educated in Virginia, where her father owned a large plantation. After her mother's death and her father's remarriage, her home life had changed. Martha and her father argued about almost everything. She could not accept her stepmother as her mother's replacement. Although no one knows for sure, it is probable Martha's grief over her mother's death caused her dislike for the plantation's new mistress. With a small inheritance from her mother's estate, Martha left the "Old Dominion" by stage and later traveled by river boat to Cincinnati where she hoped to teach. However Ohio's frontier held no demand for her cultured education.

Knowing exactly what he wanted, Chivington, in his customary fashion, wooed and pursued Martha Rollason and within a year, they married. Although marriage filled much of his loneliness with happiness, Chivington grew restless. Within two years of their wedding vows, John ventured away from the lumber business to work as an apprentice carpenter. Within a year he upgraded himself to a precise carpenter, mastering a difficult trade.

But something seemed amiss in his life. In 1843, he discovered what he sought on the banks of the Ohio River, when he attended a series of revival meetings. An evangelist there beckoned listeners to join him in the holy fight for righteousness. He preached of hell fire and brimstone and spoke of God's love. His words filled John with wonder. As he listened, John's childhood memories took him back to the first time he heard tales of good triumphing over evil from the "Good Book." Had not David killed Goliath with just a smooth stone when all seemed against him? And, in the name of righteousness, hadn't Joshua brought down Jericho's walls with blasts from his army's trumpets? Yes, those tales filled his mind and feelings came over him he hadn't felt in a long time. The spirit filled his soul and he knew he must join the Lord's sacred fight. With his devoted wife and infant son by his side, John Chivington started down his path of righteousness by joining the Methodist Church.

As the evangelist's words still echoed in his mind, John felt a stronger calling permeate his senses. He still heard John the Baptist summon him from the wilderness of unrepentance. John longed to be more than a parishioner so he asked to join the ministry. His request was readily accepted, but they offered him minimal theological training. In his perfectionist's soul, John knew he wasn't qualified to reach the frontier hamlets' citizenry. He refused his appointment by saying, "I do not propose to preach the word of God in ignorance. Until I can give a good reason for every particle of faith that is in me, I shall not enter the pulpit."[33]

Chivington studied all books of Methodist literature he could locate. He voraciously studied world history, science and economics. In the following two years, John experienced little rest. He continued his backbreaking work as a carpenter during the day and gave his total devotion to study at night. He felt blessed to have Martha by his side. As his constant companion she helped him in any way she could. Their love and respect for each other replenished their souls and gave them strength for their life of hardship. During these years, Martha gave birth to two daughters. Finally his incredible schedule of work and study ended. Late summer finally gave way to Ohio's autumn countryside. Although the days stayed fairly warm, the nights became cooler and less humid. In this time of year, when summer became a fervent memory and the earth prepared for a cold winter's sleep, John Chivington prepared for his rebirth. On a pleasant September day in 1844, the Methodist Church ordained him a minister.

---

[33] *The Fighting Parson*, p. 27.

John felt destiny fulfilled his special kinship to this calling, for had not Christ been a carpenter before He began teaching? The exhilaration Chivington felt then equaled the emotions he experienced fifteen and a half years later, as he left the pulpit to become a commissioned officer in the Union Army.

Frontiers have one thing in common, they all disappear with the arrival of settlers. Houses, schools, and churches were built from the abundance of maple and elm trees. And the multitudes of people, all coming from somewhere back east, raised families and barns. Soon those vast virgin tracts of wilderness harvested towns and cities. Often enough, the only thing these communities lacked was law and order. And the only guidance they received came from a "parson," if one could be found. Again, those in search of new towns to build pointed their wagons and lives West.

These were the communities to which John Chivington came to spread the Lord's words. His congregations soon discovered his herculean size and strength beneficial. Their new parson, devoid of fear, would fight any man or men meaning harm to the weak or underprivileged. In those foundling towns, Chivington noticed a group of individuals also seeking to bring about law and order. He admired their work as they attempted to maintain a high level of morality within the community. Chivington discovered they were members of an organization called Masons. Impressed with this group's work he eventually joined their ranks in 1846.

Two years later, in 1848, the Chivington family again followed the western roads where they settled in Quincy, Illinois. His assignment in the Illinois Conference of Methodist Episcopal Churches began as a protector of his people. He counseled, advised, refereed disputes and often became bail bondsman to those arrested. The Reverend also testified in court for them in an attempt to persuade judges to turn first offenders over into his custody. More often than not, many of those parishioners feared Chivington's wrath more than a jail cell. Overall, though, the community respected John Chivington as a leader. Even gamblers and saloon keepers, from whom he sought and received financial aid to build schools and churches, respected him.

The Reverend Chivington was a man possessed by his community and its welfare. He put his very existence into the improvement of its people, their education and spiritual guidance. In Quincy, though, Reverend Chivington ran into a situation he had never before encountered — slavery! The business of selling human

Colonel John Milton Chivington.   Photo courtesy Denver Public Library, Western History Department

bodies and the institution's ability to reach out beyond the South's boundaries astonished Chivington. Slavery now traveled north to touch the lives of those seeking to build a new country. Although Chivington had detested slavery since he first read about Moses asking Pharaoh to free his people, the Methodist Church asked its leaders not to take a stand on the issue. They feared taking sides would split the church into two factions. Since Chivington felt this detestable practice demanded political action, he agreed.

Although John stood firmly against slavery, his wife saw nothing wrong with the way it existed on her father's plantation. From what she had witnessed at home, Martha felt slavery beneficial to both whites and blacks. Her aristocratic eyes could not look beyond the color of skin.

An event in 1848 brought Chivington face to face with the problem already dividing the country. In Quincy the reverend kept attendance in his congregation open to all. One day, however, a delicate situation confronted John Chivington, pitting man's law against God's. A mulatto nursemaid who regularly attended his church changed Chivington's stance on slavery. The free blacks who lived in Quincy considered her a member of their community. They informed Chivington a deputy U.S. Marshal from Tennessee carried an arrest warrant for her as a runaway slave. Chivington sought the girl out and took her back to his parsonage for sanctuary.

Later, when the marshal arrived for his prisoner, Chivington confronted him on the front porch. The reverend stood motionless in the summer night's heat, coldly staring at the lawman. Through the undershirt he wore, Chivington revealed his massive arms and chest. Unsure of the situation, the marshal stepped forward and produced his warrants. He had come for his prisoner, the marshal said, and he advised Chivington he was authorized to use deadly force against any person interfering with his duties. Raising his voice and fists to the Tennessean he towered over, Chivington told the lawman to take his foot off the porch step. Armed with his herculean strength, he informed the marshal, he would fight for God's law, which viewed slavery as an abomination. The following moments of silence seemed an eternity for the southern lawman. He lacked the courage to take on this huge man of the cloth. Gingerly, he departed with his warrants, never to return. After this incident, Chivington became a relentless scourge on slavery's institution. His fight against servitude set brother against brother in his very own family. Chivington's brother, Lewis, was a southern sympathizer. During the Civil War, he joined the Confederate Army and was commissioned a colonel. He was killed leading his regiment in a charge at the bloody Battle of Wilson's Creek in southeastern Missouri on August 10, 1861. From that time until his death, John never spoke Lewis' name again.

As the world changed for his family, the winds of fortune beckoned them west again, this time to Missouri, where John became a circuit rider. There, he served the churches of Hannibal, La Grange and Shelbyville in eastern Missouri and St. Joseph in western Missouri. Chivington also covered Wyandotte, Kansas, where the church assigned him to minister the Wyandotte Indians. The Wyandottes settled there after their treaty with the United States in 1842. Among these people, Chivington's booming baritone voice needed an interpreter because many Wyandottes still retained their old language and customs. He created numerous ministries and brought about a peaceful coexistence between the Indians and white settlers. Pleased to discover "that the savages seemed eagerly seeking some word of God, some light in the darkness of failure to understand the Almighty"[34] Chivington continued his work until late 1854. The church then transferred him to St. Joseph. Martha was jubilant! Not only would John be home, but St. Joseph offered stability and decent education for their three growing children.

St. "Joe" did offer stability, but it also brought the slavery problem to Chivington's front door again. In the turbulent decade of the 1850's, border gangs from Missouri and Kansas raided the "free soilers'" homes. These were people who believed no one person had the right to enslave another. In some cases, border gangs shot up and burned entire towns because of the "free soilers," stand against the South's evil slave empire. More often than not, these "raiders" gave the reverend wide birth. They knew he would not scare or cower in a fight.

Chivington's stand as a "free soiler" did not make him popular in some areas along the Kansas-Missouri border. At one point, a gang of men threatened him with tar and feathers if he preached in Platte County the following Sunday. However, this fighting Reverend of Irish descent sent out his own message — he would indeed preach. The heat of that summer's Sunday seemed cool compared to the crowd's heated anticipation of the day's outcome. A group of toughs arrived earlier with an ample supply of tar and

---

[34]Ibid., p. 37.

feathers. They planned to haul Chivington off his pulpit and tar him as promised. They had a surprise waiting for them.

In the morning, when Chivington entered the church's pulpit, he set his Bible down at the lectern's center and then placed two pistols on either side of it. In a powerful voice he stated, "By the grace of God and these two revolvers, I am going to preach here today!"[35] Slowly, Reverend Chivington stepped back from the lectern a couple of paces to see if anyone possessed the courage to challenge him. As if enchanted by an ancient spell, a silence crept over the crowd gathered in that house of God. From then on, no one in St. Joe ever again threatened "The Fighting Parson" to his face. On the other hand, many of Chivington's parishioners and friends felt his life was in danger in Missouri. After some soul searching and a lengthy discussion with Martha, he finally agreed to be transferred to the arid Nebraska village of Omaha in 1856. Chivington's time in Omaha proved somewhat peaceful and productive for the church, but he grew restless.

Four years later, like the crispness of an autumn wind whose ominous journey speaks of winter's cold and famine, John Chivington, his wife Martha and their three children left the warmth of Omaha's security to follow the family compass again. It led them west to the wildest town they had ever encountered. When the Chivington's arrived in Denver in 1860, violence, murder and mayhem were so prevalent, vicious vigilante committees enforced the laws of the land.

Men went on trial for their lives in barrooms, whose jurors were drunken sots. If defendants were found guilty, they were promptly removed from the bar and hanged from the nearest lamppost or tree. Most folks joked about the common occurrences of shootings and stabbings. "You plug 'em, we plant 'em," or "you stab 'em, we slab 'em" became common phrases, along with some very strange epitaphs. John Walley, the city's undertaker, was said to have owned only one coffin. He used it to transport bodies between the barrooms and bone yard.

One of the local cemetery's tombstones carried unusually creative messages to send some of the dearly departed on their way. They read like those in the Kansas and Arizona Hell Towns:

> Here lies Lester Moore,
> Shot with six slugs from a forty-four.
> No less, no more.

---

[35]Ibid.

Another tombstone reportedly read:

> Here lies Richard Gillis
> Who was waylayed and murdered by Shotgun Thompson.
> Rest in Pieces.

With her wooden framed buildings and her streets of dirt, the infant city of Denver, born of theft and nourished by greed, greeted the Reverend John Milton Chivington in 1860. Twelve months later, Denver's citizens witnessed the presiding Elder of the Methodist Episcopal Church depart from his church for love of country.

When the distant sounds of drums and cannons were felt in Colorado after South Carolina troops fired on Fort Sumter, love of God and country became, "My God, the Country!" Without hesitation, Reverend Chivington asked Territorial Governor William Gilpin for a commission as an officer in the First Colorado Volunteers. Puzzled, Gilpin queried Chivington on why he wanted to fight. Wasn't he a man of God? The Parson replied,

> I am a man of lawful age and full sized and was an American citizen before I became a minister. If the church had required me to renounce my rights of manhood or American citizenship before I became a minister, I should have respectfully declined![36]

In 1861, the Reverend John Chivington left the church to become a major in the First Colorado Volunteers. Since that time, the memory of the "Gun Toting Parson" was forever forged in the fiery frontier beginnings of the "Mile High City" of Denver.

---

[36]Ibid., p. 65.

Territorial Governor John Evans, in later years.

Photo courtesy Denver Public Library, Western History Department

5

The Governor and His Quest

The winds of fortunes
Often blow in unexpected ways,
Men fight to build a better world
To repeat civilized man's old barbaric days.

W hen he first saw this "city," he realized, compared to Chicago or Evanston Illinois, Denver was just a mud hole nestled against the majesty of the incredible snowcapped Rocky Mountains. Though beautiful in its setting, this town filled its confines with the worst kind of rabble known to man. In his first trip west of Omaha, Nebraska, the new territorial governor, Dr. John Evans, vowed not to be mired down here for too long on his quest for a seat in the United States Senate. He had friends back east and the sooner he could get this territory into the Union, the sooner his path would open to the senate. Evans, however, encountered obstacles before he again ventured east.

For most of his forty-eight years, John Evans overcame almost every obstacle life put in his path. At five-feet eleven-inches tall and about 180 pounds, he possessed more energy and education than a score of men half his age. Before Evans left Chicago on his journey to Colorado, he'd been recognized as one of America's foremost innovators in his field of medicine, a business man, an administrator at Rush Medical College and a founder of the city of Evanston, Illinois. Before his death thirty-five years later, John Evans accomplished more than even he dared to dream. He became legendary for his part in the growth of a western empire. But he also burned scars of hatred into the hearts of the Cheyenne and Arapaho nations, whose people roamed this dominion before the white man's great western exodus.

As with many great men, Evans' life began in a log cabin, when young Rachel Evans gave birth to him on March 9, 1814. She and her husband, David, knew of infant mortality's presence, common on Ohio's western frontier of Warren County. Born healthy, this son of Quakers became male heir to his family name and farm. As though destined for greatness in the unsettled western lands, this infant inherited both his father's shrewd business sense and his mother's compassion to help the needy, ill and sick of heart and mind.

For David Evans, this child created new responsibilities. To insure his wife and child would not lack life's basic necessities, David supplemented his farm income by working in his father's auger shop. He also took any other work his neighbors offered him. Within months of John's birth, young David Evans prospered, and with his father Benjamin's help, he opened his own general store, while continuing his interests in tool-making and farming. As his business grew, so did his need for more room.

David knew his family needed larger living quarters when Rachel became pregnant with their second child. He commenced work on their new home, and in 1816 the Evans family moved. In 1820, David flaunted his four prosperous years by building a large brick home. Eventually, two other sons came into their world and their new home. Of the four boys, only the older two, John and Joel matured. The infants, Evan and Owen, died before 1821.

For the first time, John witnessed death on the Ohio frontier. Although only seven years old at the time, he remembered his father and mother's heartbreak. No matter how explained, death of infants and small children seemed so unfair. Death, as he learned, recognized no boundaries and discriminated against no one.

John had matured into a young man by the time his father relocated to Waynesville, Ohio, in 1837. David Evans began investing his money heavily in real estate, particularly in the lush, rolling hill country surrounding his Warren County farm. As his business venture proved lucrative, western Ohio's frontier began to shrink.

John Evans continued to work on his father's farm, although between the years 1834 and 1836, he was in and out of school. In his family's general store he met people from all walks of life, through the doors entered merchants, men of the cloth, traders of all kinds and marketing men from small businesses. With this diversity of people, he and his father probably met and traded with a tall, muscular, youth in the timber business. This teenage boy was born and raised in that same county — his name was John Chivington. After all, these two families lived only ten miles apart in a sparsely populated county.[37]

John Evans envisioned a life beyond what he considered the mundane existence of a farmer and store clerk. Behind his deep set eyes and gentle face, there lurked a mind craving only what could be found within schools and colleges. John excelled in school, and in 1834 he convinced his father to send him to the Hicksite School in Richmond, Ohio. After a year in Richmond, John reluctantly returned home to work for the summer.

He and his father argued bitterly about his returning to school during those hot, humid months of summer. David wanted his son to remain in the family business and John couldn't see spending the remainder of his life working a job unable to kindle his mind's creativity. Finally, they reached a compromise and John left for a Quaker college in Pennsylvania, although this too lasted a year. Young Evans' lack of respect for his school master's intellect created a problem for his return to that school. However, John's year there instilled a need within him. While in Pennsylvania, he visited all of Philadelphia's museums, dance halls, theatres and libraries.

This "City of Brotherly Love" opened John's eyes to a world he'd never known as a Quaker. Philadelphia's cosmopolitan streets were lined with well-dressed men and women. The sidewalks and cobblestone streets down which he ventured opened doors for his endless quest to see what awaited him around the next corner of this "birthplace of a nation." His imagination thrilled to what it must have been like to witness the legendary happenings within the sacred walls of Independence Hall. John's mind reeled with excitement as his feet stood where trod, a scant sixty years before, the footsteps of Jefferson, Hancock, Adams, Franklin and others. He could hear the echo of their voices raised in debate and their

---

[37]According to the Warren County Historical Society in Lebanon, Ohio, "It is probable that these two men knew each other."

speeches reverberated in his ears as he touched the foundations of freedom itself. In his mind John heard the words, "life, liberty and the pursuit of happiness," that were used to help forge the great sword of freedom. Upon the desk in that great hall, he saw where freedom's scriptures were molded with the point of a pen. He knew the laws of the land which were so eloquently spoken began from this ink's flow. Philadelphia introduced John Evans to an intellectually challenging world. And within him grew the reality he could never return to Warren County's life-style nor to his parent's religion.

The energy which guided John charged him to search his soul for a vocation both benefiting those around him and at the same time satisfying his needs. While in Philadelphia, Evans toured the University of Pennsylvania's School of Medicine. The smell of those halls instinctively and instantly led John towards the Hippocratic oath. Six months later, this son of country Quakers enrolled in Cincinnati's College of Medicine.

His two years of medical school proved academically easy. He immersed himself into the not yet scientific field of medicine. Nineteenth century illness cures were still one-tenth science and nine-tenths superstition. One of the most popular cure-alls Evans and his classmates were taught was "bleeding" a patient or by applying a living leech to them.[38] The theory behind this practice of blood letting or blood sucking came from the belief "bad blood" caused illness. If a doctor could drain out the "infected" blood a cure would follow. John learned many doctors watched Indian women to discover what roots and herbs they used in cases of vomiting during pregnancy. He read of one doctor's advice of "a decoction made from roots of Indian cup-plant to alleviate nausea."[39] Evans and the other students also heard cures for things like a simple nosebleed. The treatment called for the patient to "put the feet into water as hot as can be borne, keep them there until relieved. This draws the blood from the head."[40] They learned too, in 1833 Doctor W. Beach outlined his cure for blood in urine, "by a strong decoction of peach tree leaves" in the prestigious medical journal *The American Practice of Medicine.*[41] These medical students were also taught that

---

[38]"Bleeding" was performed by cutting a patient's skin open and letting blood flow freely for short periods of time. The less extreme method of this practice incorporated the use of living leeches. The use of leeches was last practiced in the early 1930's.
[39]*American Folk Medicine*, p. 208.
[40]Ibid., p. 188.
[41]Ibid., p. 160.

laudanum, prescribed for pain, produced a euphoric effect on patients. They were probably unaware of the addictive nature of laudanum's two main ingredients, opium and alcohol. The addictiveness to this drug became rampant after the Civil War, due to the horrendous wounds suffered by the veterans. After being on morphine and laudanum for long periods of time to ease their pain, these veteran soon found their bodies craving these drugs. This form of drug addiction became known as the "Civil War's" disease.

The anatomy class however, would challenge any man's fortitude. Nineteenth century medical students did not possess the luxury their twentieth century counter-parts take for granted. By law, no one was allowed to "will" their body to science. Finding a cadaver to study proved a delicate and secret endeavor. Doctors allied themselves with the most detestable of men to fulfill their needs — grave robbers. Who better knew the status of dearly departed than those who made their living selling off the dead? Under the cloak of darkness these men secreted their way into cemeteries with pick, shovel and crow bar to fetch their human lucre for prominent men of science. The most infamous case of body snatching at the Cincinnati College of Medicine occurred forty years after John Evans graduated. In 1878 grave robbers snatched the body of the newly departed John Scott Harrison. Harrison was unique in American History. His father was President William Henry Harrison and one of his sons became President Benjamin Harrison. After the doctors paid for his body, they took it into the medical lab and hanged it by the neck. One of the first persons to arrive the following morning and find the dangling corpse was medical student John Scott Harrison Jr.[42]

Unlike the dead he studied, John survived his studies. Financially though, he barely possessed enough capital to subsist on, and just prior to graduation, he borrowed forty dollars from his friend, Elias Fisher. However, the toils of his studies and finances seemed trivial when he finally began his struggle with the affairs of the heart. A few months before Evans earned his degree, while visiting home, he met and fell in love with Hannah Canby, the daughter of a wealthy, prominent Ohio physician, Joseph Canby. Although attractive, intelligent, and somewhat naive, Hannah was a spoiled only daughter. Her positive traits made John eager to care for her

---

[42] *The Complete Book of the Presidents*, p. 139.

the rest of her life. Before he returned to school, he asked Hannah for her hand in marriage and after the few cat and mouse games most young lovers play, she accepted. Leaving her to return to school became unbearable for John. During his remaining months at the Cincinnati College of Medicine, John filled his few free hours writing letters to Hannah. In those letters he brought forth the searching of his soul and the dreams he held for their future together. On March 3, 1838, John Evans, after completing his thesis on brain tumors, graduated a Doctor of Medicine. The young doctor now desired a practice and a home for his bride to be.

After graduation, Doctor Evans searched for a town close to home in which to hang out his shingle, but to no avail. When the town of Hennepin, Illinois, offered John a practice, his bride-to-be emphatically informed him she wasn't interested in being far from her father's household. John and Hannah quarreled, but after a time, she relented and said she would follow him. John's antici- pated position didn't work out quite as he'd planned, so he left Hennepin to set up practice in West Milton, Illinois. His practice failed there too, the city's population appeared to be extraordinarily healthy. Dr. Evans had barely established his medical practice in West Milton when he and Hannah finally married. It was December, 1838.

What started out as a dubious occupation for Dr. Evans soon proved very profitable after he and Hannah moved to Attica, Indiana. During his early years there, he converted to the Methodist faith. His practice flourished, as did his family, for two boys were born to John and Hannah: Joseph in 1839 and David in 1841.

Throughout Indiana and the medical community, the name Evans became prominent. Articles Dr. Evans wrote appeared in medical journals and his reputation as a respected doctor spread. Between 1839 and 1844, he and his friend, Dr. Isaac Fischer, worked tirelessly to establish a state hospital in Indiana. This was no easy task. In the mid nineteenth century, the mentally ill, the depressed, and the retarded along with the blind, the deaf and the mute were all treated as insane. There were no established hospitals to educate or treat these impaired human beings. The families of these people were normally charged with their care. If the families were destitute, the township or county government subsidized them for food and clothing. The familys' treatment of the "insane" in many cases was worse than death. One Illinois woman kept her brother in an open pen. Every two weeks she would clean the area, "by having neighbors tie him down while they threw buckets of water into the pen. One winter the man's feet froze, crippling him."[43]

Dr. Evans' struggle for his hospital for the insane introduced this dedicated healer into the world of politics. To acquire the monies he needed for his programs from state legislators, John Evans learned how to rally voter support by listening to a young Methodist evangelist named Mathew Simpson. One lesson he memorized, "it's who you know, not what you know."

The next few years became the most hectic he ever experienced. After he successfully lobbied Indiana's State Legislature for the building of the State Hospital for the Insane, they appointed him its first superintendent.[44] If Evans had been aware of the kind of treatment the state's wards received, after the hospital opened in 1850, he probably would not have lobbied as hard as he did for its creation. Most patients came from indigent families or from families not wanting to be bothered. They warehoused society's outcasts in the state's newest institution. During lunch and dinner hours, the institutions herded patients into large halls for inadequate portions of food. Untrained attendants abused the inmates in every way imaginable. Many were beaten, kicked, and had food forced down their throats. Others were sexually assaulted. During its first year of existence, the Indiana State Hospital for the Insane housed 134 people. There was only one recorded death. Within twenty years the institution housed 792 persons and recorded 51 deaths.[45] The mortality ratio increased dramatically, but during the first few years after its inception, John Evans concerned himself with saving life.

During the winter months, he taught at Rush Medical College in Chicago while continuing his own medical practice. In 1848 Evans moved his family and successful practice to Chicago, Illinois. However, within two years, tragedy again reared its ugly head. Three of John and Hannah's five children passed away by the year's end and in 1850, Hannah was dying of tuberculosis. Before John's eyes, his wife of twelve years wasted away, and as a physician, he remained helpless. He watched as the disease decimated her body and listened as the severity of her coughing caused her to wretch

---

[43] *A Mad People's History of Madness*, p. 108.
[44] Evans acted as a building supervisor during the construction of the hospital. He held no post there after the hospital received its first patients.
[45] *Mental Institutions in America: Social Policy to 1875*, p. 376.

time and again. He tried in vain to keep her comfortable but in those middle years of the nineteenth century, no cure for tuberculosis existed. On October 9, 1850, Hannah Canby Evans died. John, overwhelmed with grief, mourned for months.

In a letter to his father, he wrote. "Just as I was preparing for the enjoyment of life, and to return to her the reward of a faithful and devoted companionship, in which the comforts of pleasant and happy home to which she had long and earnestly looked forward, and so richly deserved, she is snatched from me and I am left alone . . . I am almost a stranger in a strange land."[46]

Hannah's death devastated John. However, after months of loneliness and depression, his fighting spirit returned. He could not sit idle. He involved himself in politics and education in Chicago and he accepted a professorship of Obstetrics at Rush Medical College. He continued to throw himself into other projects that helped raise the educational standards for the city's poor. He demonstrated his inherited business sense, investing in real estate and within the next few years, John Evans, M.D., became a very wealthy man. Wealth does not buy happiness though, and in 1853, a flame of love rekindled his heart's passion.

John met her at a friend's house in Chicago and her youth and vitality made the thirty-nine year old physician feel like he was in his twenties again. Margaret Patten Gray, though sixteen years younger than the Ohio doctor, totally captivated him with her good looks and charm. She brought back an optimism and enthusiasm to his existence that he hadn't experienced in years. The benevolence of Margaret's youth and love of life infected John's every waking moment. After a whirlwind courtship, Margaret married John on August 18, 1853 at her family's home in Bowdoinham, Maine.

With his bride by his side, Evans' next seven years resulted in one great accomplishment after another. He financed railroads in Illinois and assisted in the establishment of the first state-funded college in Illinois — Northwestern University. He also published a prestigious medical journal and founded the City of Evanston, Illinois. John's unbelievable energy equaled his inner drive to overcome any obstacle placed in his path. Driven by the challenge of deeds not yet attempted by others, the fruits of his labors were never as sweet as his tasks.

---

[46]Letter from John Evans to David Evans, January 15, 1851.

John's driving force finally carried him from the city of Chicago to the wild western frontiers beyond the Mississippi River. His years of hard work, influence and political clout finally paid off. In 1862, John Evans received a presidential appointment as a territorial governor. Evans supported Abraham Lincoln in the 1860 election for various reasons, though probably the biggest was his stand on slavery. Lincoln impressed John with his views during a speech he gave in Peoria, Illinois, in 1856. The speech made Evans remember his first encounter with this detestable practice. While on a business trip to New Orleans, Evans wrote home, "slavery can only be maintained by the most inhumane barbarity."[47]

Evans stayed active in politics because of slavery's issue, and he sought to change this injustice through the power of public office. He felt Lincoln was one of the answers to the question of ending slavery's practice. Evans and other founders of the Republican Party helped elect the "Railsplitter" as the nation's first Republican President. During his long, uncomfortable train ride from Chicago to Omaha, Nebraska, Evans felt the fates had been good to him. His journey to replace William Gilpin as Territorial Governor of Colorado began quietly, but his tenure caused the west to erupt in violence.

When Evans arrived in Omaha, he boarded a coach bound for Colorado. While riding a stagecoach on the hot, dusty Overland Trail to Denver, Evans had an abundance of time to think about what challenges lay ahead. Replacing Gilpin was not going to be easy. What John Evans knew about Gilpin impressed him — here stood a man whose appearance and life were so diverse from his own. He knew William Gilpin as a man who was either loved or hated in Colorado. And Evans knew, change would not come easy to the territory, for his concepts of governing were totally different from Gilpin's. He was keenly aware their early religious training was the only similarity they shared in life. Gilpin, also born of Quaker parents, grew up in Pennsylvania. Many in the west considered Gilpin, though a year younger than Evans, a man's man, the total personification of the rugged westerner. Gilpin, lean and muscular from his days on the frontier, still stood as tall and as straight as he had during his one year at West Point.

On the other hand, John Evans possessed the looks of a stern but gentle middle-aged school master. Not only had John inherited

---

[47]Letter from John Evans to Hannah Canby, May 28, 1842.

his father's business sense, he also inherited his father's prominent nose. He concealed a strong chin beneath the full beard he grew and wore his hair long, in the fashion of the day. It also helped cover the top half of his large ears.

Within the first sixty days of his presidency, when the Colorado Territory broke away from Kansas Territory in 1861, Abraham Lincoln appointed "Billy" Gilpin its first territorial governor. Gilpin was an extraordinary individual. During his appointment process, he received recommendations from prominent businessmen and politicians alike. His supporters sent him directly to President Lincoln. William Gilpin was an intelligent visionary who, before being sworn into office as governor, had been a soldier, explorer, writer, newspaper editor and a bodyguard for President Lincoln himself.

When William Gilpin took office as governor, he had already explored Colorado on more than one occasion. As far back as the Mexican War he had served with Stephen Watts Kearny's troops. Gilpin wore one of the many "blue coats" Black Kettle and other Cheyenne had seen at Little White Man's fort on the Arkansas in the summer of 1846.

When Gilpin served as a U.S. Army colonel in Colorado in 1847, he became well acquainted with many of the Cheyenne and Arapaho. He personally knew the chiefs Yellow Wolf, One Eye and Black Kettle. He also maintained friendships with people like Kit Carson, John C. Fremont, Ceran St. Vrain, Susan Magoffin and Little White Man. Gilpin's knowledge of the west was as vast as the country itself and he loved its ways and its people. As times and countries change so do the winds of political fortune, and in 1862, Gilpin ran afoul of Washington's powerbrokers and Lincoln removed him from office.

During his year in office, Gilpin accomplished a great deal for the infant territory. He nurtured the framework for solid development in Colorado and lit the spark of civic spirit that breathed life into the territory and gave it a vitality of its own. In order to keep the peace in the newly designed territory, Gilpin established the First Colorado Volunteer Infantry Regiment which was formed to fight any and all hostile Indians. He also vowed to keep Colorado in Union hands, for Civil War had already erupted back east. He organized the civil authority and its judicial system of law enforcement and courts. While Colorado remained a part of the Kansas Territory, inadequate law enforcement existed. Arapaho County Sheriff, Edward Wynkoop, covered too much territory and wielded too little authority to be effective within Denver's city limits. Wynkoop and the law enforcement system under which he operated were replaced with the new administration.

In May of 1862, John Evans entered Colorado Territory. By that time the Civil War in the east had already made its way west. Two months before Evans arrived, Major John Chivington of the First Colorado Volunteers won a great victory over General Sibley's Confederate forces at Glorieta Pass, New Mexico. Yes, Evans had many obstacles to overcome. Governing a wartime territory wasn't going to be easy, but John Evans was at his best when faced with monumental challenges. With Chicago a thousand miles away, John Evans set to the task of making Colorado livable for families. He knew without families and small industries, the territory would never become a state and his road to the U.S. Senate might end. His first step towards this goal began with the Indian problem.

6
The Year of Hunger

Some men hunger for food,
While others hunger for gold,
But when empty pockets prevail,
The hungry rarely grow old.

In summer's latter days, quaking aspen trees in the high country had already started their colorful change from green to gold. In 1863, Colorado's autumn arrived early. On the plains, buffalo herds began migrating east and south of the mountains as the nights turned cooler. During Governor Evans' first fifteen months in office, Robert E. Lee's brilliant Confederate victories in the Southeast made the Civil War's outcome pure speculation to Colorado onlookers.

There were still many southern sympathizers in Denver and the "Queen City's" citizens feared another attempt by southern troops to invade the rich gold and silver fields of Colorado. Other citizens were terrorized even more by a fear of the unknown. In this time of fear, in 1863, fate sent Robert North to Governor John Evans. Some say North rode a "pale horse,"[48] and he fed the fires of rumor in Denver. In the past few months, growing hostilities between whites and Cheyenne could have been avoided if ignorance had not prevailed. Rumor begot rumor until they nourished people's fear of the "unknown." Then the "unknown" took a name and it was "Indian!"

---

[48]Biblical reference to "Death." Book of Revelation Chapter 6, verse:8, "I looked and Behold there was a pale horse! Its riders name was Death, and Hell followed close behind him."

Destiny guided the Cheyenne's ordinary life-styles in a bizarre direction in the early months of 1863; it helped steer them towards a place called Sand Creek. As if ordained by "The Wise One Above," Cheyenne braves frequently made war on the Utes. Warfare for these tribes usually consisted of raids on each other, to steal horses or count coup. The trails those warriors traveled for years ran in and around the new City of Denver. Susan Riley Ashley, an early resident recalled, "One beautiful Sunday morning, during my first year in Denver (1861), I remembered being startled by a most weird and unfamiliar sound, which sent me to the door to learn its source. From there I saw a band of Indians coming up our street, and a minute later thirty or more Cheyenne and Arapahoes passed by, holding aloft on poles five freshly — taken Ute scalps."[49]

Indian agent Samuel G. Colley found it almost impossible to keep the two tribes from warring with each other. The Utes, he reported, were observed on numerous occasions heading east to raid the Cheyenne and Arapaho. These raids etched grisly sights in the minds of new white settlers, which only helped imbue the perception, "all Indians were savages." These attacks reinforced one culture's lack of understanding for the other, placing one more stone in the wall of ignorance.

One incident, though, left a group of curious Arapaho horrified. On the outskirts of Denver, the Indians heard a loud, clanging noise. As they approached the sound, they discovered its source was a wagon full of pots and pans. Sitting in the wagon was an old woman, known as "Mother Maggard." Tall and lanky, "with an abundance of homeliness, with tangled locks of faded carrot hue and store teeth poorly set on misfit frames," Mother Maggard was no shrinking violet.[50] Among those who witnessed the following events was Wolfe Londoner, a young man destined to become mayor of Denver. With absolute authority, after seeing the Indians and fearing an imminent attack, Mother Maggard ordered everyone not to shoot. The old woman then grabbed a large skillet and began to furiously wave it around her head and began to scream at the Indians in an attempt to scare the Arapaho away. However, she succeeded only in making them more curious. Cautiously, the Indians ventured closer to this unusual sight. Mother Maggard knew shooting at the Indians would only end in disaster for the

---

[49]Susan Riley Ashley, "Reminiscences of Colorado in the Early Sixties," *The Colorado Magazine*, Vol. XIII 1936, pp. 222-223.
[50]January 1907 issue of the *Sons of Colorado* magazine.

people of her wagon. Nervously, she contemplated her next move. Thoughts of being killed or worse, being ravaged, raced through her mind. Out of desperation, she removed her false teeth and snapped them together with her hands at the astonished Arapaho. They had never seen false teeth before and fled in terror before the old toothless woman, whom they left standing and laughing in the wagon.

Unfortunately, not all incidents were humorous. Earlier in 1863, Cheyenne and whites clashed in several minor skirmishes. In Weld County, near the mouth of the Cache de la Poudre River a Cheyenne raiding party looted some local residents of their food and belongings, but harmed no one. A detachment of First Colorado Volunteers, under the command of Lieutenant Hawkins, investigating the incident reported, "The Indians talk very bitterly of the whites — say they have stolen their ponies and abused their women, taken their hunting grounds, and that they expected would have to fight for their rights."[51]

In another event, at Fort Lyon, a soldier tried to trade a bottle of whiskey for a Cheyenne woman. When the brave who took the whiskey refused to surrender the woman, a fight broke out. During their scuffle, the trooper drew his revolver and shot the Cheyenne through the arm. William Bent reported the incident saying, "the matter created great confusion among the Indians, but was finally settled without a fight."[52]

Not all problems were created through violence; corruption was in full bloom that year. William Bent and others reported Agent Samuel Colley and his son Dexter numerous times to authorities. They, along with trader John Smith, traded the Indians their own annuities. What they didn't trade, they sold for profit to others. One stationmaster's wife at Fort Lyon, Mrs. Julia Lambert, described how Mrs. Colley baked pies from the Indian's annuity flour and sold them to soldiers on the post. Even though the Cheyenne later substantiated these incidents, no charges were ever filed against the Colleys or Smith.

Free wheeling traders, both white and Mexican, sold junk goods and bad whiskey to any Indians they found willing to trade with them. Living under the white man's agency conditions left the Cheyenne and Arapaho nearly destitute. Hunger and disease

---

[51]Annual Report of The Commissioner of Indian Affairs, 1863, p. 240.
[52]"The Chivington Massacre," March 3, 1865, p. 93.

forced many young warriors to leave their reservation's designated areas in search of food and other necessities.

Reports sent to Washington from the army about corrupt Indian agents seemed to magnify the growing problem. In March, a delegation of chiefs from the Cheyenne, Comanche, Arapaho, Kiowa and Caddoe tribes was invited to visit President Abraham Lincoln. To the Indians this trip embodied the spirit of hope. They felt it imperative to strengthen the bonds between whites and themselves. Representing the Cheyenne were Lean Bear, Standing in the Water and War Bonnet.

Ten years before this peace delegation gathered, Lean Bear attempted a war of his own. As a young warrior visiting Fort Atkinson, Lean Bear took hold of a young officer's wife's hand to admire her ring. Her husband suddenly rushed up and viciously struck the Cheyenne with a bull whip. Lean Bear leaped upon his horse and rode off to the Cheyenne village haranguing the young warriors to join him in a war with the whites. He painted his face black and white, which told his people he was ready to live or die that day. Fortunately, cooler heads prevailed and the chiefs calmed everyone down. And now Lean Bear himself was a chief and peacemaker. He and the others began their first journey on the great "iron horse," to preserve what little peace existed in the land of the Cheyenne.

In Washington D.C.'s cold, humid climate of late winter, when Lean Bear and the others arrived by train, they were dumbfounded by the city's vastness. They marveled at the U.S. Capitol's huge dome, still under construction, and stood in awe of the Great White Father's massive lodge. The number of whites they observed, though, completely overwhelmed them. They saw thousands of civilians, but were frightened by the fraction of the 90,000 "blue coat" soldiers they saw, stationed in the nation's capitol to prevent a Confederate invasion.

After taking in many of the wondrous sights of the white man's "Capitol" and shaking hands with the many dignitaries who gave them tobacco, Lean Bear and the others were taken to meet President Abraham Lincoln. Lean Bear remembered the tall chief of whites. His face was kind, but his eyes were sad. During their visit, the Cheyenne chief and others pledged to keep the peace. In return the "Great White Father" presented them with gold friendship medals. But while these Indians were being shown the white man's wonders and receiving medals, the situation in Colorado significantly worsened.

The commander of Fort Larned, Colonel Jesse Leavenworth of the Second Colorado Volunteers, patrolled the Santa Fe Trail and he desperately needed more manpower. At one point, while on patrol, he ran into a numerically superior band of Comanches within thirty miles of Fort Larned. Fortunately, the Comanches were peaceful, but his luck could have easily changed because of the large amount of whiskey being sold to Indians throughout the frontier.

For a while, his lack of manpower seemed to be Leavenworth's smallest problem. On the morning of July 9, 1863, a drunken Cheyenne named Little Heart provoked an incident that could have caused a major war. Little Heart had returned to the fort to buy more whiskey but an Osage guard barred his entry at the fort's gates. Undaunted by this obstacle, Little Heart tried to run down the protesting Osage with his horse. In self defense the guard shot and killed the young Cheyenne.

The fort, surrounded by Apache, Arapaho and Kiowa Indians, left Leavenworth in a very precarious situation, and not knowing which tribe the dead man belonged to, he

> sent runners out for all the scouts to return to the post and called a council of all the chiefs. By 8 a.m. all the chiefs (principal chiefs) were here. As I had told the runners to inform the chiefs I did not want any braves or other Indians to visit the post, all kept away except the Kiowas, they could not be governed by their chiefs and came in strong force, and very much excited; more so than any other Indians I ever saw. Upon an examination of the dead Indian by the chiefs, it was found to be a Cheyenne; as they happen to be in small numbers, and we happily escaped a collision for the moment. What may happen is impossible for me to say.[53]

These incidents and others left Leavenworth furious with Colonel John Chivington for withholding so many of his troops in Denver. Leavenworth complained to his friend and subordinate Lt. Colonel Samuel Tappan at district headquarters, then in command at Fort Lyon. Chivington's refusal to send Leavenworth the additional men he requested presented a dangerous situation for those who traveled the Santa Fe Trail.

---

[53]*Rebellion Records,* Series 1, Vol. XXII, Part II, pp. 400–401.

Chivington became livid when he found Leavenworth had gone over his head. He wrote definite instructions to Tappan,

> you will not, therefore, send or go with your forces to Larned, or indeed out of the district, except for temporary purposes . . . Colonel L. has no authority to call for troops from this district, and will not have."[54]

Chivington's young adjutant, Lieutenant Silas Soule delivered his message.

The trouble between Leavenworth and Chivington came to a head when Lt. Colonel Samuel Tappan, disobeying Chivington's orders, finally sent reinforcements to Fort Larned. Chivington immediately removed Tappan as Commanding Officer at Fort Lyons and eventually had Leavenworth dishonorably discharged from the army. [55]

Chivington's wrath did not stop with Leavenworth. He immediately ordered thirty-three year old Major Scott Anthony to replace Tappan at Fort Lyon. Before coming to Colorado, Anthony, as a "jayhawker," had also fought border gangs in "bloody" Kansas. His first cousin was Susan B. Anthony, a nationally known human rights leader. Like so many others of his time, Anthony, overcome by "gold fever," departed Kansas in spring of 1860. After his arrival in Denver he was commissioned an officer in the First Colorado Volunteers by Governor Gilpin. He too served with distinction during the Battle of Glorieta Pass.

The Indians at Fort Lyon did not like or trust this man. They soon learned that, unlike his famous cousin Susan, Scott J. Anthony was not a compassionate human being. He displayed his obvious lack of humanity a short time after his arrival at Fort Lyon. Having heard of the Cheyenne and Arapaho's plight of disease and starvation, Anthony wrote, "The Indians are all very destitute this season, and the government will be compelled to subsist them to a great extent, or allow them to starve to death, which would probably be much the easier way of disposing of them."[56] These events, culminating with the arrival of North, Lean Bear's killing and the murder of Ward Hungate's family, started the existing clash of two cultures towards the road of total disaster for the Cheyenne and

---

[54] *Rebellion Records*, Series 1, Vol. XXII, Part II, pp. 172–173.
[55] A subsequent review of the facts by Judge Advocate Holt reversed the Dishonorable Discharge to an Honorable Discharge.
[56] *Rebellion Records*, Series 1, Vol. XXII, Part II, p. 571.

Arapaho. And the appearance of Robert North in John Evans' office diminished any chance of peace.

Robert North was said by some, to be crazy and by others to be a liar. There were still others who said he was a hero and an adventurer. Historically, little is known about this blonde, blue-eyed renegade. North had been raised by the Arapaho since childhood and, unlike George Bent, was born of one culture — the white, but he lived his life almost entirely in the Indian culture. Though never totally accepted by either race, North lived in a time when these two cultures were about to collide head on and he sought a safe middle ground. He held a basic philosophy: when with whites, be white, and when with Indians, be an Arapaho!

When North arrived at Governor Evans' office in Autumn of 1863, he brought a tale of pure terror to every white man who heard it. North, who was illiterate, dictated a statement which spoke of his presence when the Sioux, Cheyenne, Arapaho and the Kiowa held a great Medicine Dance. During the dance, he said, the Indians agreed to stay friendly until they could obtain the necessary guns and ammunition to destroy all white invaders. Even more astounding than his tale was the fact no one ever tried to verify it! Evans immediately ordered Agent Colley to stop the issue of guns and ammunition to all Indians.

While North was creating panic in Denver, diarrhea and whooping cough were devastating Indian children in alarming numbers. With their annuities being misappropriated and game and ammunition almost non-existent, the year of 1863 became known to the Cheyenne and Arapaho as "the year of hunger."[57]

To his credit, Evans did attempt one council with the Indians, but it failed for numerous reasons. The most obvious was his total lack of knowledge about these people's customs. With disease and hunger running rampant in their villages, the tribes hunted during spring and summer for whatever game they could find for their winter survival. Those precious seasons could not be wasted on talk with whites who used liars as their spokesmen. Evans insisted on using John Smith as an interpreter. Both the Arapaho and Cheyenne disliked and distrusted this man they called "Lying John Smith."

Had Evans used his influence to stop the corruption in the Indian Agency and relied on men like "Little White Man" and had

---

[57] *The Arapahoe — Our People*, p. 170.

he used common sense in investigating unfounded rumors of war, Lean Bear might have seen another season. And had the Governor tried to understand the cultures of the Cheyenne and Arapaho, people who wanted peace with the whites, the Hungate family may have lived well beyond that late spring day of June 11, 1863.

7
The Decree And The Dead

It's never too late to learn to hate
And to follow another's will.
For in Death's land there's a waiting Fate
Who will teach you how to kill.

O n a knoll just west of the village, men in blue waited like a dark shroud ready to cover the morning light. The frosty breath of both men and horses rose eerily and silently in that chill and as it climbed above them, it vanished like an apparition in the waning darkness of night. For the majority of men present, this was the moment they had waited for. But there were also those who were in attendance through no choice of their own.

Robert Bent and James Beckwourth were both forcibly taken by Chivington and his troops and compelled to act as guides to the Cheyenne and Arapaho village below them on Big Sandy Creek. Members of the Third Colorado Volunteers abducted Robert Bent, William's oldest son, from his ranch at gunpoint. Earlier, Chivington's troopers removed the ill, sixty-nine year old Beckwourth from his Denver home, when they left the city. The Colonel threatened to hang him if he did not participate in this military venture.[58]

---

[58]"The Sand Creek Massacre," p. 74.

There were soldiers present, however, who had joined this command in hopes of preventing a tragedy. Captain Silas Soule was one. Angered by Chivington's plans, his former adjutant rode with the troops in an attempt to persuade his former commander not to attack the village. Time and again, he and others tried to reason with him, but their attempts were futile. Chivington's only response was, "Damn any man who is in sympathy with the Indians!"[59]

In Soule's mind, there must have been a sheer sense of urgency to stop the transpiring tragedy. Surely, this wasn't happening. In his mind's eye, Soule must have kept seeing the words "if only." If only Governor Evans and Chivington had listened at Camp Weld, maybe many of the recent dead would still be alive. If only the Governor's decree had not been issued, maybe reason could have prevailed. And if only Major Wynkoop had not been relieved from command at Fort Lyon, maybe the volunteer rabble of the Colorado Third would not be sitting on this knoll. If only . . . if only . . . if only . . . must have echoed through his mind, only to be met by a resounding, "where?" that came from the depths of his throat. Where was Wynkoop? Could he do anything in time to stop the culminating madness of the last two years? And in those last terrible moments as he waited and prayed for a reprieve for the doomed people below him, Soule must have asked himself "why"? If he and Ned Wynkoop could change their ways of thinking about the Cheyenne and Arapaho, why couldn't Evans and Chivington?

Meanwhile, as Chivington's men poised themselves above the village in the cold November dawn, a lone stagecoach, escorted by a small cavalry detachment, made its way to General Curtis' headquarters in Kansas. The one military man who tried to change the collision course of two races of people, from which racial history would never recover, was the lone passenger. Unaware of the unfolding tragedy on Big Sandy Creek, Major Edward "Tall Chief" Wynkoop made his auspicious passage to Kansas, a journey in vain.

Born just twenty-six years before to well-to-do parents in Pennsylvania, Edward W. Wynkoop arrived in the untamed west in 1856. Like many other young men in search of high adventure, tall, good-looking and good-natured, "Ned" Wynkoop soon shed his "greenhorns." When Wynkoop crossed the Mississippi River and proceeded West, he discovered Kansas an endless land of prairie grass and violence.

---

[59]Senate Executive Documents, p. 47. The testimony of Lt. Cramer.

These new, rugged lands west of St. Louis offered the dreams of a lifetime to those willing to risk their lives to fulfill them. As a test ground in the fight against slavery, "Bleeding Kansas" offered the law abiding little protection, save the gospel according to "Smith and Wesson," "Samuel Colt" and their six children of lead. In the land beyond these warring plains were the Rocky Mountains, and according to folks who had been there, beyond those mountains there was "no God." Only those who had traveled the Santa Fe Trail during the past few years and the mountain men and conquistadors before them had ever laid eyes on this country before.

Tales flourished about "painted savages" who roamed throughout this land. Stories of murder, rape and depredation were synonymous with the names of these people: Pawnee, Osage, Kiowa, Arapaho and Cheyenne. To the new intruding whites, these Indians were to be feared, hated and not trusted under any circumstances. These stories were told as often and in almost the same breath as rumors of great fortunes awaiting those who were foolish enough to seek treasures in this precarious promised land. Death's dwelling place was called "Kansas" and beyond those windswept plains lay Hell itself. For in the frozen cathedrals of the Rockies it was said, if the mountains didn't kill you, the Utes who lived there would!

Within two years of Edward Wynkoop's arrival, the Territorial Governor of Kansas appointed him Sheriff of the newly formed Arapaho County. His job consisted of keeping the peace, housing prisoners and serving legal papers in an area covering what is now almost all of eastern Colorado and on into the Rockies. Upon leaving Kansas in autumn of 1858, Wynkoop's first assignment was to accompany the Leavenworth-Lecompton gold rush party to a place where the Cherry Creek joins the Platte River. When he journeyed to his newly appointed jurisdiction by horseback, Sheriff Wynkoop brought along his .36 and .45 caliber cap and ball pistols, a badge and a learned hatred of people he had never met.

After weeks of traveling hundreds of miles, Wynkoop and his party finally reached their destination. Nestled against the snow-capped Rocky Mountains were the townships of Auraria, Montana City and St. Charles. Wynkoop's men were greeted by the noise, smells and sights of these bustling little mining camps which were founded by the twin-edged knife of hope and greed. This same knife forged the makeup of Wynkoop himself, as well as Leavenworth and William Larimer. Within twenty-four hours of his arrival, Wynkoop and eight others jumped the St. Charles' township claim, threatening Charles Nichols, the sole caretaker of the site, with a "rope and a noose" if he didn't leave as quickly as possible.

The following day Wynkoop threw all of his time into keeping the peace. Fighting, shootings, and stabbings brought on by the onslaught of drunken and disorderly men filled these townships. He discovered much of the town directed their violence toward the peaceful Arapaho who had camped there for decades.

When Little Raven, a chief of these people, saw the never ending flood of whites coming from the east, he stated, "It will be a very hard thing to leave the country that God gave us."[60] Within the next few months, the Arapaho slowly moved their campsites, as more buildings were erected in this new city of Denver. And with the buildings and new-comers came churches and preachers.

In 1860, in the time the Cheyenne called "The Fat Moon" (April), Arapaho County became a part of the newly formed Colorado Territory. With the arrival of a new territory and a new parson, the Reverend John Milton Chivington, the consequences caused by both man and event forever scarred the memories of the Cheyenne and Arapaho. The paths of men and events intertwined like a rope, yet each strand remained a separate entity unto itself.

Sheriff Wynkoop's first meeting with this huge parson probably occurred at the Criterion Bar. Denver's saloons oftened doubled as church and courtroom. The two men met as Chivington came to give spiritual comfort to a condemned man. At first, this 260 pound man of God impressed Wynkoop. Intelligent and outspoken, he seemed totally fearless in these rough and somewhat lawless mining camps. Within four years of this meeting, though, Wynkoop's admiration for this man turned to pure hatred.

When the Civil War erupted twelve months after their initial meeting, Wynkoop resigned his job as Sheriff of Arapaho County and was commissioned an officer in the First Colorado Volunteers. Chivington too changed his occupation. He laid down his churches' cloth and picked up an officer's commission and a U.S. Army sabre. To both of these men, slavery was an abomination and the Union must be preserved at all costs.

One year later, both men participated in the Battle of Glorieta Pass. After John Chivington's victory there in 1862, the army promoted him to colonel and Wynkoop to major. The following year, Wynkoop struck up a friendship with a young adventurer,

---

[60]*Denver—Mining Town to Metropolis,* p. 15.

Major Edward Wynkoop in 1861.   Photo courtesy Denver Public Library, Western History Department

Chivington's adjutant, Silas Soule. He too was recently promoted to captain. With their promotions in rank came new responsibilities.

In 1864, Major Wynkoop and Captain Silas Soule were ordered to take command of a dilapidated fort in southeastern Colorado named Fort Lyon. When they arrived on May 9th, the fort's condition and that of the men stationed there astounded them. The majority of the personnel suffered from scurvy. The army failed to resupply this outpost with any of fresh fruits or vegetables for months. Rank enjoyed no privileges when this disease came to visit. Scurvy had afflicted the officer whom Wynkoop relieved of command. Due to the lack of vitamins C and A in his diet at the fort, Major Scott Anthony's eye pigmentation permanently turned red. From that day on, both the Cheyenne and Arapaho referred to Anthony as "Major Red Eyes." If it were possible, the fort itself seemed to be in worse condition than the men stationed there. The crumbling walls offered almost no protection from the elements, let alone a hostile attack by marauding Indians. Wynkoop must have felt he had just been given the proverbial "armpit" of the west for his new assignment.

The fort's military objective was to cover General Curtis' right flank at Leavenworth, Kansas. Upon arriving, Wynkoop contacted Chivington and asked instructions about a course of action to take against the Indians. He notified Chivington there were Cheyenne in the area, but they had committed no hostile acts. On the last day of May, Chivington sent the following reply to Wynkoop: "The Cheyennes will have to be soundly whipped before they will be quiet. If any of them are caught in your vicinity kill them, as that is the only way."[61] Without question, Wynkoop obeyed his orders. Exactly one week after Wynkoop's arrival at Fort Lyon, the army murdered a curious and peaceful Cheyenne chief. His name was Lean Bear.

On a pleasant May morning on the Smoky Hill River, nearly fifty miles northwest of Fort Larned, Lieutenant George S. Eayre and his Independent Battery of Colorado Volunteer Artillery encountered a massive Cheyenne hunting party. History is uncertain as to who saw whom first, the army or Indians. What was certain though, surprised by this huge body of Cheyenne, Lieutenant Eayre made his troops ready for battle.

While Eayre shouted orders to his men, an artillery sergeant named Fribbley noticed the Cheyenne displayed no hostile actions.

---

[61] *Rebellion Records*, Series I, Vol. XXXIV, Part IV, p. 151.

In fact the amazed sergeant observed what appeared to be two of their chiefs riding towards him shouting a greeting. The chief uttering the greeting wore a gold medal around his neck. Fribbley's comprehension of the Cheyenne language was nil, but it was obvious he and the other man broke off from the main body of Indians. They were peaceably trying to communicate with him and Lieutenant Eayre. Sergeant Fribbley accompanied the chief with the medal back towards his troops and his commanding officer. When the chief and the other Cheyenne were about twenty feet from Eayre, the young Lieutenant ordered his troops to open fire. A volley of bullets returned Lean Bear's greeting. The two Cheyenne were shot from their horses. Soldiers quickly rode up and shot them again as they lay on the ground. Lean Bear and Star lay dead on the dew-covered grassland near the cool waters of the Smoky Hill River. He had ridden forward to show Eayre his papers and medal the "Great White Father" gave him in Washington D.C.

Eayre notified Chivington, "400 strong" Cheyenne attacked him, but after a seven and a half hour fight he had "succeeded in driving them from the field. They lost three chiefs and twenty-five warriors killed; the wounded I am unable to estimate. My own loss is four men killed and three wounded."[62]

The Lieutenant greatly exaggerated his report to Chivington; he had made no attempts to communicate with Lean Bear. Eayre and his men killed three Cheyenne and wounded three others. The Cheyenne had killed four of his men and wounded three others as reported. The reality of the incident was Lean Bear's murder outraged the onlooking Cheyenne and Eayre and his men were forced to retreat. The pursuing Indians chased Eayre all the way back to Fort Larned's safety. Chivington had ordered Eayre and his men to search out and kill all Indians they encountered; if they found their villages, to burn them. Eayre and his men had followed these orders successfully for over a month. Often fact becomes half-truth or fiction when glory is involved, and glory's storytellers are never accurate when vanity blinds them.

To many Great Plains Indians the storyteller's symbol is the spider. His webs spin their people's cultural stories so that the gods of the four winds may see those tales and spread them throughout earth's domain. The web of stories surrounding the spring of 1864 soon reached out to entangle almost all of eastern Colorado's population and those dwelling in western Kansas.

---

[62] *Rebellion Records*, Series I, Vol. XXXIV, Part I, p. 935.

When the tale of Lean Bear's death spread amongst his people, warring forays of Cheyenne and Arapaho soon became much more dangerous than the symbol of fear the spider portrays among whites. Kansas received the brunt of the punishment, but fear of imminent Indian attacks heightened in Colorado to panic proportions in less than a month after Lean Bear's death.

When panic peaked, it did so with swiftness and ferocity in an Arapaho raid and it festered with the insensitivity displayed by Denver's "good" people. About midday on June 11, Ward Hungate and his hired man, Miller, took a break from their search for stray cattle. Miller noticed smoke rising from the direction of Ward's ranch house. Without hesitation, both men raced their horses to a high point overlooking Hungate's ranch. Ward couldn't believe his eyes. His stock had already been driven off and he watched as flames consumed his ranch house. Miller yelled at Hungate to leave immediately for Denver. Nothing could be done for his family or ranch. But Ward Hungate knew the thirty mile trip to get help would take hours. He could not bring himself to leave. Somewhere below him were his wife and his two small daughters. As he urged his horse towards the house, Hungate told Miller to ride for help. Ward knew only marauding Indians could have caused the devastating sight below. All he knew and loved was in or near the inferno of his house. While Ward Hungate continued his downward charge towards an unknown fate, Miller fled to Denver and safety. The Hungates were never seen alive again.

The following day, a man identified only as Mr. Johnson and a small group of men from a nearby mill discovered the Hungate tragedy. About a hundred yards from the house, Johnson found the bodies of Mrs. Hungate and her two children. She had been stabbed

> in several places and scalped, and the body bore the evidences of having been violated. The two children had their throats cut, their heads being nearly severed from their bodies. Up to this time the body of the man had not been found, but upon our return down the creek, on the opposite side, we found the body. It was horribly mutilated and the scalp had been torn off.[63]

Four Northern Arapaho were responsible for the Hungate's ghastly deaths, but the people of Denver further profaned their

---

[63] *Rebellion Records*, Series I, Vol. XXIV, Part IV, pp. 97–99.

tragic demise by placing their bodies on public display. In a shed, where the Denver Civic Center now stands, the good citizens of Denver witnessed the horrors about which Governor Evans had attempted to warn Washington, D.C. And for "one thin dime, one tenth of a dollar," the local folks could pay for the thrill of touching the dead, mutilated rancher, his wife and two small children. They kept the Hungates on this morbid display for almost two days. Late spring's heat and the lack of ice for the four decomposing bodies made their burial imperative.

Towards evening on the last day of the Hungate's grisly display, panic ruled the Queen City. A frightened rancher, who thought he had seen Indians, came riding into town at full gallop. Down East Fourteenth Street he rode, screaming, "Indians are coming; Indians are advancing on the town to burn and massacre. Hurry your wives and children to places of safety!"[64]

According to Susan Riley Ashley, the news spread like a strong wind and it sent the people of Denver "in every stage of dress and undress"[65] running for the protection of the town's most fortified buildings: The U.S. Mint and the Commissary Building on Ferry Street. The story kept the majority of Denver's citizens nighttime guests in those two buildings, but by sunrise, the nonexistent hostiles had still not appeared.

Three days after the Hungate murders, Governor Evans sent a telegraph of panic directly to Secretary of War Edwin Stanton, which read,

> Indian hostilities on our settlements commenced, as per information given you last fall. One settlement devastated 25 miles east of here; murdered and scalped bodies brought in today. Our troops near all gone. Can furnish 100-days men if authorized to do so, to fight Indians. Militia cannot be made useful unless in the U.S. service, to cooperate with troops. Shall I call a regiment of 100-days men or muster into U.S. service the militia?[66]

In his request, the Governor failed to mention the "settlement" consisted of a young family of four.

In the following two months, before Evans received permission to raise his troops, the tensions endured by settlers and plains Indians

[64]Susan Riley Ashley, "Reminiscences of Colorado in the Early Sixties," *The Colorado Magazine*, Vol. XIII 1936, pp. 219–230.
[65]Ibid.
[66]*Rebellion Records*, Series I, Vol. XXXIV, Part IV, p. 330.

reached their limits. The stress even caused men like William Bent to see the inevitable eruption of an all out war between the two races. The shooting of an Indian would bring the death of whites in retaliation and soon troops were on patrol at regular intervals, not just to look for Confederate raiders, but more often to hunt down and kill any Indians they could find.

On August 11, 1864, Governor Evans issued a proclamation to the citizens of the Territory of Colorado. It read, in part,

> I, John Evans, governor of Colorado Territory, do issue this my proclamation, authorizing all citizens of Colorado, either individually or in such parties as they may organize, to go in pursuit of all hostile Indians of the plains, scrupulously avoiding those who have responded to my said call to rendezvous at the points indicated; also, to kill and destroy, as enemies of the country, wherever they may be found, all such hostile Indians.[67]

His proclamation also gave all such citizens a reward of sorts, saying they could keep all property belonging to dead Indians as an inducement to kill more. The Governor's proclamation further offered,

> all such parties as will organize under the militia law of the Territory for the purpose to furnish arms and ammunition, and to present their accounts for pay as regular soldiers for themselves, their horses, their subsistence, and transportation, to Congress, under the assurance of the department commander that they will be paid.
>
> The conflict is upon us, and all good citizens are called upon to do their duty for the defence of their homes and families.[68]

The same day Evans' proclamation appeared in the *Rocky Mountain News*, Secretary of War Stanton notified Evans of his approval for a 100-day regiment. The proclamations and orders passed on August 11th pleased John Evans. His road to the Senate seemed a little clearer.

However, two hundred miles southeast of Denver, an ironic twist of fate unraveled in the form of an official letter. Unbeknownst to whites and Indians alike, another strand of the spider's web

---

[67]"Massacre of Cheyenne Indians" in Report of the Joint Committee on the Conduct of War, Part III, 47. (Subsequent references to this document will be cited as "Massacre of Cheyenne Indians".)
[68]Ibid.

ATTENTION!
INDIAN
FIGHTERS

Having been authorized by the Governor to raise a Company of 100 day

U. S. VOL CAVALRY!

For immediate service against hostile Indians. I call upon all who wish to engage in such service to call at my office and enroll their names immediately.

Pay and Rations the same as other U. S. Volunteer Cavalry.

Parties furnishing their own horses will receive 40c per day, and rations for the same, while in the service.
The Company will also be entitled to all horses and other plunder taken from the Indians.

Office first door East of Recorder's Office.

HAL SAYR.

Central City, Aug. 13, '64.

Posters for 3rd Colorado Volunteers.

Photo courtesy Colorado Historic Society

reached out to entangle them. About fifteen Arapaho, under Neva's leadership, spotted what they sought near the mouth of Sand Creek — a soldier, an ordnance sergeant named Kenyon. He had ridden out alone from Fort Lyon in search of stray horses.

Neva hallooed the sergeant and attempted to show him a letter he held from Indian Agent Colley. Neva waved the letter at Kenyon, but the sergeant thought he was being attacked. Naturally, when he turned his horse around to race back to Fort Lyon, the Arapaho gave chase. Kenyon's thoughts at the time didn't include the fact these Indians sought to parlay. He rode as hard as his horse would carry him, back towards safety. When he reached his destination he blurted out his report to Major Wynkoop. He told his commanding officer he'd been chased by a band of fifteen Indians.

Wynkoop didn't waste any time. He ordered thirty men into the saddle to hunt and do battle with the Arapaho. He divided the troops into two squads, led by Lieutenants Cramer and Baldwin. Approximately five miles east of the Fort, Cramer caught sight of the Arapaho. When Neva realized communication with these whites was impossible and only conflict would arise with an armed squad of soldiers, he fled. Cramer assumed the retreat meant the Arapaho lost their will to fight. The young Lieutenant and his fifteen men chased Neva and his warriors for almost twenty miles. When Cramer finally caught up with the Arapaho, he had only six men accompanying him. The nine troopers' horses had faltered from the high paced race across the plains.

The peaceful Neva finally lost patience with these white men and turned to give Cramer a fight. As he and his warriors turned, they spotted the remainder of Cramer's troops encroaching on their position, and again the Arapaho veered off towards safety. The Arapaho suffered four wounded warriors in a running fight that took place over a four mile stretch of prairie. Indian Agent Colley had written the letter Neva carried and it stated the Arapaho sought peace.

Back in Denver, recruitment for what formed the Third Colorado Volunteers was pursued by the Queen City's worst denizens. Drunkards, rowdies and Indian haters signed up by the dozens for the 100-day military excursion. It gave them an opportune time to collect a few scalps under Union colors. The anger and hate boiling in the hearts of Colorado whites continued to rise and overflow like molten lava as atrocities committed by both white and Indian spread throughout the land. There are lulls before the storm though and sometimes a cool wind can soothe a scorched land or an aching heart. Such a wind arrived in the Cheyenne time of the "Cool Moon" (September).

As the omnipresent wind of late summer fanned the prairie grass of southeastern Colorado, Major Edward Wynkoop's standing orders at Fort Lyon fanned a burning legacy of hatred. His orders from Chivington read: "kill all Indians." When three of his men disobeyed those orders, Wynkoop became livid. Not only had they not killed the Indians, they actually had the audacity to escort them back to the fort as prisoners! This event forever changed Ned Wynkoop — the man.

The incident began on September 4th, as three troopers of the First Colorado Volunteers were traveling to Denver to be mustered out of the army. A short distance from the fort, these combat veterans encountered three Cheyenne, two men and a woman. The troopers' initial reaction was to draw their weapons and fire upon these Indians. But one of the Cheyenne men made peace signs as he pointed to a letter he held above his head. The troopers cautiously approached the Cheyenne and after a while escorted them back to the fort. After Wynkoop finally cooled down, the Major sent for John Smith, who was present in the fort.

Wynkoop asked Smith if he would act as an interpreter. The Major decided to obtain what information he could collect from these "savages" in hopes of discovering something useful. Wynkoop watched curiously as Smith began talking with one of the Cheyenne. He soon discovered he was in the presence of a Cheyenne chief named One-Eye and his wife. He learned the other Cheyenne was a warrior, named Min-im-mie. Wynkoop demanded an explanation for One-Eye's visit to the fort. The Cheyenne chief then produced two very similar letters.

Both letters were written by William Bent's second son, George, who was presently in Black Kettle's Village. The letters, addressed to his father and to agent Colley read:

Cheyenne Village, August 29, 1864

We received a letter from Bent [William], wishing us to make peace. We held council in regard to it; all came to the conclusion to make peace with you, providing you make peace with the Kiowas, Commandoes, Arapahoes, Apaches and Sioux. We are going to send a messenger to the Kiowas and to the other nations about our going to make peace with you. We heard that you have some prisoners at Denver; we have some prisoners of yours which we are willing to give up, providing you give up yours. There are three war parties out yet and two of Arapahoes; they have been out for some time and expected in soon. When we held this council there were a few Arapahoes and Sioux present. We want true news from you in return. (That is a letter.)

The letter was signed: "BLACK KETTLE and other Chiefs"[69]

One-Eye also told the startled Major there remained over two thousand Cheyenne and Arapaho along with about forty lodges of Sioux camped on the headwaters of the Smoky Hill River. They sought a military spokesman to meet with their chiefs to discuss the possibilities of a peace treaty.

Wynkoop's initial reaction to One-Eye's offer was skeptical. Was this a trick to lure his troops out to be massacred by the Cheyenne and Arapaho or was this "savage" sincere? He pondered his next move carefully as destiny intervened with his decision. Edward Wynkoop's personal integrity and his sense of fair play soon overshadowed his learned hatred for these people. After a council with his officers, the young commandant of Fort Lyon agreed to meet the multinational chiefs at their camp. He would lead a 127-man patrol and take two small howitzers on the expedition. However, Wynkoop insisted that One-Eye, his wife and Min-im-mie remain with the troops as hostages. In case of treachery, they would be quickly executed.

Without reservation, One-Eye calmly agreed. In his conversation with Wynkoop, One-Eye stated the Cheyenne never broke their word and if they did, he would not care to live any longer, for in his people's language, the word for "lie" did not exist.

This Cheyenne chief baffled the young Major because he appeared fearless and stood tall during the interrogation inter-preted by Smith. Wynkoop later recalled, "I felt myself in the presence of superior beings . . . that I heretofore looked upon without exception as being cruel, treacherous, and blood-thirsty without feeling or affection for friend or kindred."[70]

Two days later, Wynkoop and his troops left Fort Lyon, feeling uncertain of their fate. He certainly felt the risk necessary to rescue any white prisoners. He hoped to become instrumental in bringing

---

[69]"The Sand Creek Massacre," p. 169.
[70]"Wynkoop's Unfinished Manuscript," p. 28.

a cessation of hostilities on the western frontier. The Major, his troops and prisoners rode for three days. On the fourth day, in what is now western Kansas, he dispatched Min-im-mie with a message to Black Kettle and other chiefs of his impending approach. On the fifth day, Wynkoop and his men were greeted by a sight which caused the hair on the nape of their necks to stand on end. As they neared the headwaters of the Smoky Hill, they met 500 Cheyenne and Arapaho warriors armed with bows, arrows, lances, rifles and revolvers. This small army of Cheyenne outnumbered Wynkoop's small force, almost four to one. As they sat on their ponies on a hill above them, the Indians shouted taunts and jeers at Wynkoop's wide-eyed soldiers of the First Colorado. The Cheyenne appeared to be forming for battle.

Wynkoop turned to his men and commanded them to defend themselves. As his men began to form a circle, the major alone continued to advance. He sent One-Eye ahead with the same message he gave Min-im-mie and reminded the chief he still held his wife hostage.

One-Eye rode his horse towards the warriors located on a ridge above Wynkoop and spoke with them. He quickly returned to the Major and stated Black Kettle indeed still wished to talk of peace. But the war cries and whoops being shouted by the Cheyenne made Ned Wynkoop very uneasy about his decision to follow One-Eye. He now prayed there really wasn't a word in the Cheyenne language for "lie." The darkness brought no rest for the 128 men from Fort Lyon. It only covered the heat and stress of the day. The adrenaline pumping in their veins caused sleep to elude their weary eyes.

The following morning at about nine o'clock, to Wynkoop's dismay, even more Cheyenne ominously greeted his troops than on the previous day. He couldn't believe the sheer magnitude of warriors before him. These people were not present to fight, though, for among them were their great chiefs: Black Kettle, Bull Bear, White Antelope and One-Eye himself. Accompanying the Cheyenne chiefs, there rode a man Wynkoop had never met — William Bent's son, George.

Wynkoop had heard of Bent, who'd recently returned to Colorado after being pardoned by Union troops in Missouri. The white military infrastructure had been put on alert about his return. They considered him dangerous. To the army, he was a classic example of a real threat to western civilization, a young, educated half-breed, who had fought against the Union after learning white guerilla tactics and now living among the Cheyenne.

This picture of Bent was fairly accurate. He had abruptly left the St. Louis school he attended when the news of Fort Sumter's surrender reached Missouri. During the uproar that followed the news, southern sympathizers attempted to secure St. Louis for the Confederacy, but were beaten back by William Bent's old friend Frank Blair and Captain Nathaniel Lyon. Caught up in the unfolding epic of the Civil War, seventeen-year-old George Bent immediately joined a Confederate unit, Colonel Green's cavalry regiment. It didn't take long for the war to reach him. When Union forces invaded western Missouri, Green's troops engaged and defeated them at Wilson's Creek. Ironically, Nathaniel Lyon became the Union's first commander to be killed in the war. William Bent's second fort, which Edward Wynkoop now commanded was named in his honor.

Later, George Bent fought with distinction in the battle of Pea Ridge and survived Grant's siege of Corinth, Mississippi. But Union forces captured him while he attempted to escape that city's fate. George Bent's return to Colorado had been very peaceful, and he surprised Wynkoop by his accompanying his mother's people. Bent was here acting as an interpreter for the Cheyenne. They did not trust John Smith's words. Representing the whites along with Wynkoop stood Silas Soule and Lieutenants Cramer and Phillips.

Black Kettle opened the council by asking Wynkoop why he brought so many men and the two howitzers; he asked if he had come to make war. He brought the men for protection, he replied, in case of treachery, as he had never before spoken to the Cheyenne.

The council began and Wynkoop spoke with the Cheyenne and Arapaho for hours. He told the assembled chiefs, there was much to discuss and he did not wish to deceive them; he was not a "big enough white chief" to offer the Cheyenne peace terms. Wynkoop then read Governor Evans' proclamation to the chiefs. He declared he would do everything in his power to arrange another council of peace, for he was presently acting entirely on his own volition.

The leader of the Dog Soldiers, Bull Bear, spoke up next. He said he had tried to live in peace with the whites for a long time, but started fighting again when they had killed his brother, Lean Bear, almost four months ago. He was angry and considered the whites to be people without honor. Many there agreed with Bull Bear's words. Yet One-Eye spoke up in defense of Wynkoop. He told the council the Major had genuinely risked his life to open up communications, just as he, One-Eye had when he journeyed to Fort Lyon carrying the letters from William Bent and Agent Colley.

The Arapaho spoke next, venting their point of view. Both Left Hand and Little Raven talked in much the same way others had before them, echoing Bull Bear's belief the Indians wanted peace, yet peace seemed impossible with the white man.

During the entire council, Black Kettle sat cross-legged, erect and silent. When all of the others finished speaking, Black Kettle gathered his blanket and rose to his feet. Eloquent and yet forceful, Black Kettle told Major Wynkoop he had always wished for peace, but peace was difficult to maintain when there were both good and bad whites and Indians. He blamed the whites for the fighting because they had forced the Cheyenne and Arapaho from their native lands. Then Black Kettle detailed the atrocities committed by both sides and how one begat the other until the present crisis was born. He volunteered to free the white prisoners held captive only if the whites would do the same with any Indian prisoners. The council ended at approximately two o'clock in the afternoon.

Following the council, the curiosity between the two races became infectious, and yet both the Indians and the soldiers remained wary of each other. A few minor mishaps occurred, but for the first time in many months, these antagonists met each other and survived the day without anyone being killed or wounded. As the sun turned its light toward the western horizon, Wynkoop, Soule, and Cramer all rode from the headwaters of the Smoky Hill River, forever changed.

On the following morning, the Arapaho chief Left Hand and several of his men surprised Wynkoop when he and the troops were returning to Fort Lyon. The first of the white prisoners promised for release accompanied the chief, a woman named Laura Roper. Left Hand also carried a message from Black Kettle saying he would appear the next day with more prisoners. Left Hand and his people would remain as hostages with the soldiers until Black Kettle arrived.

True to his word, Black Kettle returned with the prisoners his people held. There were three white children ranging in ages between four and seven years. Black Kettle told the dumbfounded major there were two more white women held captive, only they were not in the immediate area. These women would be returned later. He also informed Wynkoop a third captive white woman had hanged herself in a Cheyenne camp.

Wynkoop's gamble on the expedition proved successful. Not only had he won freedom for the four white hostages, but he had held council with chiefs of the Cheyenne and Arapaho. As he and his men escorted the hostages back to Fort Lyon, Wynkoop must have hoped these first steps would shorten the long journey towards lasting peace. His immediate plan involved bringing these chiefs back to Denver. He hoped Governor Evans would council with these men, thus ending the hostilities plaguing the land. But, unbeknownst to the major, at the very moment of his journey to Denver, more people were falling in harm's way.

General James Blunt, commandant of the Upper Arkansas district decided to "steal a march on the red devils and give them a good chastising, which is the only thing that will do them some good — a little killing."[71] Blunt left Fort Larned with four hundred men, including Major Scott "Red Eyes" Anthony. They scouted and located a quiet village of Cheyenne and attacked. Nine Cheyenne died. Blunt's losses were one dead and seven wounded.

While Blunt's troops attacked a mere seventy miles away, Wynkoop and the Cheyenne and Arapaho chiefs continued on their two hundred dust-filled miles by horse and wagon to Denver. Once they arrived, they were greeted by a somewhat curious and angry crowd of spectators. The major truly believed Black Kettle and the others would be protected if they arrived in Denver under the colors of a large American flag fastened to their wagon.

Upon receiving word of Wynkoop's arrival, Colonel Chivington and particularly Governor Evans initially refused to speak with the Indians. After some coaxing, though, the governor reluctantly and angrily agreed to meet with Black Kettle and the others at Camp Weld, located just outside of Denver.

Evans, Chivington, Wynkoop, Soule, Shoup, Cramer and John Smith were among those who attended the council held on September 28, 1864. Representing the Cheyenne and Arapaho were Black Kettle, Bull Bear, White Antelope, Neva and Left Hand. Others present included Ute Agent Simon Whiteley and an attorney named Amos Steck.

---

[71] *Rebellion Records*, Series I, Vol. XLI, Part II, pp. 670–71.

Moke-Tavato (Black Kettle).   Photo courtesy Colorado Historic Society

Black Kettle spoke first, telling Evans he had received his circular and had abided by its terms. He continued to say he never wanted to fight the whites, he had always befriended them. He eloquently told Evans,

> You are our father; we have been traveling through a cloud; the sky has been dark ever since war began. These braves who are with me are all willing to do what I say. We want to take good tidings home to our people, that they may sleep in peace . . . I have not come with a little wolf's bark, but have come to talk plain with you. We must live near the buffalo or starve. When we came here we came free without any apprehension, to see you and when I go home and tell my people that I have taken your hand and the hands of all the chiefs here in Denver, they will feel well, and so will all the different tribes of Indians on the plains, after we have eaten and drunk with them.[72]

Evans listened with "closed ears" though, and accused the Cheyenne and Arapaho of being in alliance with the Sioux to make war on all whites. He further told Black Kettle he held no interest in peace at that time, for soon the plains would swarm with many soldiers. The Indians, he told the chiefs, would be driven from the land altogether.

Defending his people's position from Evans' harsh words, Bull Bear spoke up and said he would personally fight against the Sioux in trying to keep peace, if that's what was necessary. He said there was no truth to rumors an alliance existed against the whites. He and the Cheyenne came to talk of peace, but no one in authority seemed willing to listen.

Chivington spoke up next. His words echoed the threats of war when he said,

> I am not a big war chief, but all the soldiers in this country are at my command. My rule of fighting white men or Indians is, to fight them until they lay down their arms and submit to military authority. You are nearer to Major Wynkoop than anyone else, and you can go to him when you are ready to do that.[73]

From the spoken words at this council and on the words written in Governor Evans' proclamation, Black Kettle and the others were promised, if they rode to the nearest fort and lived in peace, no harm would befall them. The Cheyenne and Arapaho felt at ease at

---

[72]"The Sand Creek Massacre," pp. 213–217.
[73]"The Sand Creek Massacre," pp. 213–217.

the end of the council. So much so, they decided to remain in Denver with Wynkoop for several days calming the fears of citizens and farmers. They even posed for photographs. Soon, they would return to the vastness of eastern Colorado on their long, dusty journey back to Fort Lyon.

Black Kettle and Wynkoop developed a deep friendship on their return trip. With each mile and every word, the two men found a respect and an intimate communication which was spoken from the heart. That in itself transcends all words. In their sojourn across Colorado's great plains Wynkoop told the old Chief about himself and his family back in Pennsylvania. In return, Black Kettle revealed the details of his life to his new friend. Fascinated by the old man's tales of his early life on the plains, Black Kettle astonished Wynkoop when he divulged he was not a true Tsis Tsis Tas. The old chief informed Wynkoop he was a Sutai. His people had come to the Cheyenne a long time ago from the northeast. They spoke the same language, but in a different dialect. Black Kettle was not one to brag, but he did reveal the details of his life as a warrior through his interpreter, George Bent. Wynkoop listened as the old man talked and yet he couldn't imagine this gentle peacemaker as one of the fierce warriors he had witnessed only days before. Wynkoop's ignorance of Cheyenne customs was evident when he said he assumed the position of chief of this nation of people was a hereditary honor. He listened and he learned as the old man talked.

In the five day journey back to Fort Lyon, Wynkoop learned Black Kettle's father, Swift Hawk Flying, was never a chief. His wife bore him three sons and a daughter. As a young man, Black Kettle became a good warrior who led several war parties against the Kiowas, Comanches, Apaches and Utes. Wynkoop could see the pain in the old man's eyes as the chief told him how he lost his first wife in a fight with Utes in the summer of 1848. But he also saw the pain slowly fade as Black Kettle spoke of his marriage into the Wotapio clan of Cheyenne. Wynkoop's stereotyped picture of how "Indian Chiefs" came to power was shattered when Black Kettle told him of his election to chief in 1850, after the death of Bear with Feathers. He also informed the major, he was never a "head" chief of the Cheyenne. In their culture, they did not exist. He quickly educated Wynkoop that his people elected a total of forty-four chiefs in all of the clans, though not all were equal. Black Kettle explained there were four principal chiefs and four chiefs from each of the ten bands of people, so all would be equally represented in the Council of Chiefs. These men, Wynkoop learned, were elected "chiefs" because of their diplomatic abilities and not for their warlike qualities. A chief put the welfare of others, especially widows and orphans above himself. Quarrels or acts of personal vengeance for offenses committed against him forbade a chief's involvement. His role was a peacemaker's. A "War Office" in the tribes did not exist amongst chiefs. The warrior societies took care of war. Black Kettle informed his young friend the leaders of the great warrior societies were often mistaken for "chiefs," but these warriors could never be chiefs as long as they were in the "society." In those early autumn days, Wynkoop learned much about his new friend. His friendship with Black Kettle endured until the old chief's death four years later.

Somewhere along their first trail together, before their journey to Fort Lyon ended, Major Ned Wynkoop lost his bigotry and became a different man. In Cheyenne custom, Black Kettle bestowed a new name upon his friend: "Tall Chief." Wynkoop witnessed another side to these people he had always been taught to fear and hate. Like a caterpillar whose body lay in darkness, Wynkoop's mind emerged from its cocoon of ignorance and saw the beauty of a world he'd never stopped to look at and it brought forth old lessons to his mind — old Sunday school lessons which spoke of "judge ye not, lest ye be judged." And with those old lessons of life came new responsibilities. "Tall Chief" Wynkoop sought to make the frontier a safe place for Indians and whites alike. The former peace officer became a peacemaker.

Shortly after Wynkoop arrived in Fort Lyon, Black Kettle and the other chiefs held another council. They organized runners to inform the other tribes scattered over the vast prairie the Cheyenne wanted peace. Soon afterwards, an exodus of Indians traveled from the barren plains to Fort Lyon's gates. When they arrived, many needed medical attention and food. Summer's hunting had been very bad.

Wynkoop took peace's initiative and offered aid to all who arrived at Fort Lyon. He heard the sounds of battle now give way to the music of laughter. He witnessed Cheyenne and Arapaho women escort their families to the fort for the first time. Children's tiny smiles and laughter broke down hatred's barriers even among some of the toughest soldiers. Unfortunately, Wynkoop soon discovered all was not well. For some, children's laughter cannot penetrate bigotry's deep-seated roots of ignorance. Notes filtered from Fort Lyon to Chivington's desk reported Wynkoop allowed Fort Lyon to be overrun by his new found friends, the Indians. According to the colonel's sources, the Cheyenne and Arapaho were permitted to camp outside the gates. During the day, Chivington was told the Indians had total access to Fort Lyon. Chivington's anger grew with every dispatch he received from the fort's commandant. The colonel wasn't happy Wynkoop's peace project was proceeding so well. He had a war to fight! With the peace initiative succeeding, Governor Evans questioned Chivington about his immediate plans. Evans felt peace might make him appear foolish. The Third Colorado was mustered to fight Indians and by the God of War Chivington worshipped, they would fight Indians! Their first chance for war arrived during the "Moon When the Water Begins to Freeze on the Edge of Streams" (October).

Not all of the plains Indians chose peace. The Sioux were the most warlike, as were some bands of Cheyenne Dog Soldiers. They continued to raid, kill and plunder any whites wandering into or settling on their grasslands. The same held true of many whites, who roamed the land in search of Indian plunder and scalps. Many of these marauders used the governor's proclamation as a license to murder. These roving bands never asked the innocent victims they murdered if they were "hostile."

On the tenth day of October, Captain David Nichols, commander of the Third Colorado Volunteers, received word a small band of Cheyenne were camped near a bubbling spring, just south of the bluffs, overlooking the Platte River. There, he found two Cheyenne lodges. Nichols took forty of his troops and charged down on the unsuspecting Indians, killing six warriors, three women and a fourteen year old boy. They also captured ten ponies and one mule. All of the Indians were scalped and mutilated. The "Bloodless Third" had just drawn their first blood.

When word of this atrocity reached Wynkoop, he, Black Kettle, One-Eye and White Antelope struggled furiously to keep the fragile peace from shattering. But they could not control those beyond their reach and in the time of the "Freezing Moon" (November), the fruits of peace began to wither on vines grown from malice.

On November 5, 1864, Major Scott Anthony astounded Major Wynkoop when he arrived with orders from General Curtis to relieve him of command. He angrily demanded to know who was responsible? The answer was Chivington. Whatever it took, Edward

Wynkoop vowed to fight this preposterous transfer. Wynkoop knew of Anthony's hatred for Indians, and to place him in command of this fort amid a fragile and tenuous peace was irresponsible! Wynkoop remained at the fort for almost three weeks collecting letters of confidence from all of his officers and overseeing a smooth transition during the change of command. When he finally departed for Kansas, he carried a tale to General Curtis few white men would believe.

On November 26th, on his journey to fight for his reinstatement, Wynkoop was unaware others also travelled the cool November plains. After conferring with Colonel Chivington about his immediate plans for the Cheyenne and Arapaho problem, Governor Evans decided a journey to Washington, D.C. would be in his best interest. He wanted to be far away from Colorado while Chivington carried out his solution. The Colonel's first step was for Anthony, as Fort Lyons' new commandant, to banish all Cheyenne and Arapaho from U.S. Government property. Anthony informed Black Kettle and the others they would be safe if they camped near Sand Creek and if they flew an American flag over their village. Anthony also informed the chiefs to send their warriors out to hunt, as winter was fast approaching.

On November 28th, just two days after his departure from Fort Lyon, Wynkoop encountered No-ta-nee, an Arapaho warrior he knew. Black Kettle chose No-ta-nee and two other warriors to alert his friend, a war party of two hundred Sioux were in the area and he should beware.

On this same day, John Smith, Private David Louderback and a teamster headed for the village at Sand Creek with a wagon load of trade goods. George Bent and his half brother, Charlie, were already in the village visiting their mother's people.

That evening an army of 700 men, commanded by a giant of a man riding a large mule, stole their way through the darkness of November's star-chilled night. Just before the first light and dawn, these men in blue stood on a knoll west of the village at Sand Creek. And there they waited, like a dark shroud ready to cover the frosty morning's light.

8
Death's Black Cape

Between the first light and the dawn,
He charged his army down
And put the village to the sword,
And in blood, his glory found.

It was not unlike other autumn mornings in Colorado's eastern plains. The darkened sky had not yet yielded to the sun, and night's chill still held morning's air in her grasp. Smoke rising from village fires seemed to reach up in silent praise to herald this dawn's arrival. For all was still on Big Sandy Creek's banks, on that frost-covered morning of November 29, 1864.

At least five Cheyenne clans and ten lodges of Left Hand's Arapaho were camped here for the winter. Though most of the village's warriors had gone buffalo hunting for winter's food supply, there remained a sense of security at Big Sandy. Black Kettle's people were told their safety against attack by the army or any whites was insured as long as a large garrison-sized American flag (six foot by twelve foot) flew over their village. The stillness quieting this November's morning was much like the calm before a storm. But the violence following the tranquility and beauty of this day, forever changed the ways of the Cheyenne and Arapaho.

To those who observed the beauty of November's dawn, it offered a quiet respite from the drudgery of everyday work. Yet no eloquence was spoken of the Cheyenne and Arapaho women's morning duties. Their day began before first light as they gathered

Overlooking massacre site from west knoll at Sand Creek.

firewood to keep the night's fire burning warm in order to cook their families' breakfast. Infants and small children were cared for as their needs required. And youngsters old enough to help were given their daily tasks. Those responsibilities were fulfilled, regardless of weather, for "The People's"[74] welfare. Though their families and village were of utmost importance, their hospitality to visitors was famous. On November 29th, there were white visitors in their midst — Private David Louderback, trader John Smith his son Jack, and a teamster named Clark. They had arrived only two days earlier to promote trade with the "friendlies" in the area.

On their third day in the village, Louderback and the others awoke to a pleasant morning, but they heard a sound from over the horizon. It was ever so soft at first, as though the wind's rhythm with mother earth had broken the serenity of autumn's morn. The village dogs heard it — the horses too. The distant sounds of pounding hooves echoed through the village like a rolling clap of thunder. Some of the women and children thought the rumbling noise was a herd of buffalo. But old Yellow Wolf knew the sound to be something else . . . horses . . . white man's horses. Private David Louderback was enjoying breakfast in his lodge, when a Cheyenne

---

[74]"The People" or "Our People" is how the Cheyenne referred to themselves.

woman entered and said "a heap of buffalo" were coming. Moments later, a chief entered and told the private there were many soldiers approaching their village. Louderback immediately left his lodge to investigate the commotion stirring in the village. What he witnessed caused his blood to run cold. There on a hill, poised to strike were Chivington's troops. He hastened Jack Smith to get him a horse, but there were none available. The women had already taken the village's small pony herd to a safe place. The presence of those soldiers represented a threat to one of the tribe's most prized possessions.

Thinking their horses safe, the Cheyenne now came out of their lodges as the rumbling noise came closer. On a knoll west of their village, Black Kettle and White Antelope saw the gathering troops and they urged their people not to panic or run. The chiefs beckoned their people to the village's center, where the American flag was unfurled. Black Kettle called for his people to remain calm, reminding them the flag protected their camp. There was no danger. They were unaware that Death had come this day. And he came to the Cheyenne and Arapaho as a vile, perverted visitor.

With his troops poised for action, Colonel John M. Chivington ordered his artillery set up. He methodically rode amongst his troops urging them to "remember our wives and children murdered on the Platte and Arkansas."[75] At one point, old Jim Beckwourth heard Chivington say, "I don't tell you to kill all ages and sex, but look back on the plains of the Platte, where your mothers, fathers, brothers and sisters have been slain, and their blood saturating the sands on the Platte."[76] The orders by Colonel Chivington and Colonel Shoup were simple: there were to be no prisoners! On that cold November day, between the first light and dawn, the bugles sounded attack. Morning's fragile veil was forever torn when Chivington's artillery rained down its carnage upon the village.

With the first sounds of battle, George and Charlie Bent ran from their lodge. They were astonished to find the village under attack. As they came out into the open, they discovered most of the village was in panic. People of all ages ran, not knowing where to go or which way to turn.

Charlie Bent stayed in camp to see if the attack would cease. It did not. Charlie and old John Smith's son, Jack, later surrendered

---

[75]"The Sand Creek Massacre," pp. 258–259. The testimony of James P. Beckwourth.
[76]"The Sand Creek Massacre," pp. 258–259. The testimony of James P. Beckwourth.

Eastern artist's conception of Charley Bent.

Photo courtesy Colorado Historic Society

to Jim Beckwourth and soldiers they knew from New Mexico. They later regretted their decision.

Meanwhile, George Bent raced back to his lodge and retrieved his weapons. Armed, he ran west towards the sand hills' protection. Once he arrived there, he found a group of middle-aged Cheyenne men. They organized what little fire power they possessed and made a short stand at this location until a cavalry troop overran their position. Fleeing from this new threat, they jumped into a dry stream bed above the Cheyenne camps. Before they reached safety, however, they ran headlong into another company of cavalry. They opened fire on Bent and the others as they rode up on the opposite bank of the stream. Faced with a company of cavalry on either side of them, the Cheyenne had one choice — run for their lives through the stream bed's deadly gauntlet of gunfire.

Many people had preceded George Bent's race for life. What he and his Cheyenne companions witnessed on their run was horrible — old men, women and children, "lying thickly scattered on the sand, some dead, and the rest too badly wounded to move."[77] And as though the Third Colorado Volunteers were a nightmare come true, their never ending presence continued to pursue Bent and his party. November's frost-laden air burned their lungs with each breath they took as they ran for two miles. After racing around an obstacle course of the dead and dying, Bent finally reached a place where the river banks were very high and steep. Exhausted, he stopped and found a large group of Cheyenne who had also found shelter here. Older men and women hastily dug pits and holes into the frozen ground. Like giant moles, they burrowed for protection into those banks.

While viewing the recent excavated earth works, a force hit George Bent that knocked him face first into the earth. He remembered the sand in his mouth tasted cold and bitter as his mind tried to comprehend what had happened to his body. Soon a warm liquid covered his lower limbs as a hot searing pain permeated his very being. The realization he had been shot through his hip seemed to culminate the day's madness. Bent struggled and then managed to tumble into one of the holes, already filled with men, women and children. The day's freezing temperatures did one positive thing for George Bent. It froze the blood from his wounds and kept him from bleeding to death.

---

[77] *The Life of George Bent*, p. 152.

As the wounded Bent took cover in the hole, Chivington's troops surrounded their position. Worked into a killing frenzy, the soldiers poured murderous fire into the besieged Cheyenne shelter. Fortunately the holes offered more than enough protection. The troops stayed there until darkness again covered the day. Under night's cover, this band of half-naked survivors escaped and fled north.

Earlier, Private David Louderback, dressed in his uniform shirt, trousers and socks, fastened a white handkerchief to a stick. While he held his flag of truce high, Louderback and John Smith, dressed in civilian clothes, approached Chivington's troops. When they were about a hundred and fifty yards from the soldiers, members of Colorado's Third opened fire on them. Like the Cheyenne and Arapaho around them, Louderback and Smith were now under attack. As they ran for their lives, dodging bullets and shell bursts, Smith heard some of the troopers yell at each other, "shoot that old bastard." Louderback and Smith found temporary shelter in the same lodge in which they'd spent the night.

Louderback, protected only by lodgeskins, kept looking out the entrance,

> watching for Colonel Chivington. I saw him crossing the creek, at the lower end of the village. I watched him until he came up within forty or fifty yards of the lodge, and I hallooed to him, calling him by name, and he told me to come on, that I was all right, calling me by name. I went out to him, and in going out a man fired at me. I asked the Colonel what they were firing at me for, and he turned around and told them to stop firing. He then told me to fall in the rear of the command, that I was all right. I told him to hold on a minute, the lodge was full of white men, pointing a lodge out to him in which John Smith was."[78]

Smith, his son, Jack, Charlie Bent, Clark and Louderback were temporarily out of harm's way.

Black Kettle could not believe what was happening. He also made a white flag of truce and hoisted it on his flagpole, underneath "Old Glory." Chivington's men ignored the Sutai chief's gesture and charged down on him. Black Kettle grabbed his wife, Medicine Woman, and ran for their lives. They too followed the same creek bed through the same gauntlet of lead George Bent and the others barely survived. After a short while, Medicine

---

[78]"The Sand Creek Massacre," p. 335. The testimony of David Louderback.

Woman stopped and fell limp. She had been shot by the soldiers. Black Kettle saw she did not move as the sickening "thud" sounds made by their bullets continued to hit her body. He wanted to stop, but knew any pause in his flight meant death. He continued his run up the creek to where his people hid in the pits.

When night came, the old chief crept out to where his wife had fallen. After thoroughly searching through the dead and dying, he found her — alive! Although shot nine times, Medicine Woman clung tenuously to life. Black Kettle carried her back to safety and then he and Medicine Woman also vanished under the cover of darkness to seek help.

When the morning first exploded into gunfire, White Antelope emerged from his lodge with his arms raised and shouted in English, "Stop, Stop!" But, the carnage continued. When he realized it was hopeless, he stood tall and folded his arms and began to sing the Cheyenne Death Song;

> Nothing lives long,
> Only the earth and the mountains.

Although unarmed, seventy-five year old White Antelope was shot down and killed. A soldier dismounted from his horse and took out his knife. He then scalped the old chief. He also cut off White Antelope's nose, ears and private parts and bragged he was going to make a new tobacco pouch from the freshly severed genitalia.

Above the shooting and the cannon's roar, Robert Bent heard the screams of women and children. George's oldest brother was Chivington's prisoner.[79] He watched helplessly as his mother's people were butchered. During the carnage, he witnessed five women hiding under a bank. When the soldiers came up to them, they showed themselves and begged for mercy, but the troopers shot them all. On another bank, one woman was lying

> whose leg had been broken by a shell. A soldier came up to her
> with drawn sabre. She raised her arm to protect herself when
> he struck, breaking her arm; she rolled over and raised her
> other arm when he struck breaking it, then he left without
> killing her.[80]

---

[79]Ironically, it was Robert Bent who helped George's prompt release from a Union prison camp in St. Louis, A friend of George's spotted Robert in town on business and told him of his brother's incarceration. Robert went to some officers in the regular army who were friends of William Bent. They arranged for Bent's pardon and George returned to Colorado with Robert.

[80]"The Sand Creek Massacre," p. 185. The testimony of Robert Bent.

Robert also witnessed a group of about forty women run to a gully for protection. When the soldiers approached, the women sent a young six-year-old girl out with a white flag. He remembered the sight of this child as she was shot in the head by a soldier. The others were also killed. He watched in silent rage as soldiers raped, scalped and mutilated the women — one young mother was found with her unborn child cut out and lying beside her.

Twenty-four year old Mochi, also called Buffalo Calf Woman survived that day, but her duties as woman ended. She watched in horror as her grandfather, father and new husband were all killed. Then, one of Chivington's soldier's came for her. Though young and pretty, she fought like a cornered cougar as he tried to tear away her clothing. She broke free from his grasp and shot the soldier dead, using a buffalo gun two white gold seekers had given her grandfather. Five years before, her grandfather had saved them from starvation on the Smoky Hill trail. On that 29th day of November, Mochi was reborn a Cheyenne warrior. For the next thirteen years, the five foot six and three-quarter inch, one hundred thirty pound woman lived both a warrior's and a mother's life.

Old Yellow Wolf was eighty-five years old on this last day of his life. The November morning brought horrible deaths for him and half of his Hevhaitaniu Clan. The soldiers mutilated Old Yellow Wolf much the same way they had butchered White Antelope. He knew "The Wise One Above" would greet many of his children's tasooms rising from Big Sandy's frost-laden ground.

During the morning's attack, Little Bear awoke early and left his lodge to find the pony herd's location. His brother-in-law, Tomahawk, had hidden the herd the night before as a safety precaution against Cheyenne enemies. As he approached the area where the horses were supposed to be, he found they were gone. As he searched for them, another Cheyenne, Kingfisher, surprised him with the speed with which he ran towards him. Breathlessly, Kingfisher told him white soldiers had just run off their herd.

After hearing this, Little Bear ran to a lookout point which surveyed the Fort Lyon Trail. Incredulously he watched as the soldiers left with the herd. He and Kingfisher then ran as fast as they could back to a village already under attack. Dodging bullets and cannon fire, Little Bear raced to his lodge and grabbed his bow, quiver of arrows, his war bonnet and shield. The thick of the battle occurring now surrounded him. With his weapons in hand he too headed for the stream bed so many before had followed. He too saw the dead and wounded as he ran through the troopers' deadly hail of fire. The shooting was so intense by the time Little Bear reached the pit's safety, all of the feathers in his war bonnet had been shot out. Unbelievably, he was untouched.

When the fighting subsided, Little Bear searched the creek bed for survivors. What he found made his mouth go dry. Then like a summer storm's flash flood, rage and hatred surged in him, drowning out all of his other emotions. Revenge consumed his thoughts, leaving no room for compassion. All of the dead had been mutilated. Even the wounded had been scalped. One old women was found wandering about and "her whole scalp had been taken off and the blood was running down into her eyes so that she could not see where to go."[81]

The magnitude of this carnage sickened many of the soldiers and scouts who later testified in the military and Congressional hearings. What followed made First Lieutenant James Olney of the First Colorado Cavalry nauseous and disgusted. He observed three women and five children, who were prisoners,

> in charge of some soldiers; that, while being conducted along, they were approached by Lieutenant Harry Richmond, of the Third Colorado cavalry; that Lieutenant Richmond thereupon immediately killed and scalped the three women and the five children while they (the prisoners) were screaming for mercy . . .[82]

At one point in the beginning of that slaughter, Captain Silas Soule ordered his men NOT to fire on any of the Indians. Towards the massacre's frenzied peak, he positioned his men between Chivington's troops and fleeing Cheyenne, so the Indians could not be fired on. For this act of defiance, Chivington never forgave Soule.

Like devils born from Hell, the Third Colorado Cavalry, commanded by Colonel George L. Shoup, commenced the whole-sale slaughter and mutilation of men, women and children. They severed women's breasts and made them into scurrilous trophies. The pubic areas of females of all ages were cut out as a gruesome reminder that "nits grow into lice." The shooting lasted for about eight hours, but the carnage continued into the night. Chivington's troops killed about one hundred thirty-three Cheyenne and

---

[81] *The Life of George Bent*, p. 154.
[82] The Chivington Massacre, Affidavit of James Olney, April 20, 1865, p. 61.

Arapaho. Ninety-eight of the dead were women and children. And death confined itself not just to the killing fields.

That night young Jack Smith, who surrendered with Charlie Bent when the attack began, briefly sat in a lodge with his father, John, and old Jim Beckwourth when a group of about fifteen soldiers from the Third Colorado appeared. About the time they entered the lodge, old John Smith heard a voice beckon him outside. As he did, a pistol was fired through an opening cut in the lodge and his son, Jack Smith, was shot in the head.

Charlie Bent was next on their list, but New Mexican soldiers camped with Chivington knew the Bent family well. They prevented Charlie's execution. With the help of Jim Beckwourth, they hid Charlie for the remainder of that bloody night and released him the following day. What happened next had far reaching consequences. After witnessing the mass slaughter of his mother's people and his narrow escape from his own execution, Charlie Bent renounced his white heritage and became the scourge of every white person in the eastern plains of Colorado, Kansas and Nebraska.

The 29th day of November was now over, but the darkness that fell was not the night. It was Death's black cape. It draped late autumn's sky into mourning's color and its landscape of soft white and brown hues was forever changed to red.

9
Escape and Retribution

The quiet of the prairie
Was shattered by the sounds of war,
And a land was murdered on that morn,
When the guns and cannon roared.

O nly the wind's sound broke nighttime's stillness, as it moaned through the sage and prairie grass. The escaping Cheyenne and Arapaho made the only other sounds penetrating the frozen evening, as they sought refuge from the army and the weather. Glowing like a million incandescent candles, the stars filling this western sky guided the half naked survivors from Sand Creek's slaughter. Each mile seemed a hundred as the cold, wounded Cheyenne and Arapaho trudged their way north to seek help from their other clans.

Unsure of his own fate, George Bent pondered his next steps and wondered about his half brother Charlie's whereabouts. Unbelievably, Bent walked much of the trip with a rifle ball still imbedded in his hip. Eventually warriors from Black Kettle's camp found him. These outriders were part of a hunting party the army purposely sent off before their attack on the village. From a distance these warriors watched the desperate fighting, but were powerless to help.

101

Little Bear and other warriors who were in Black Kettle's camp, acted as a rear guard for those who escaped to the prairie's cold, harsh safety. He watched as the wounded were either carried or made their own way across the open plains. There were few blankets and fewer buffalo robes to warm those Cheyenne. They were unaware of what danger lay ahead or if they were being followed by Chivington's troops. Above all else, they dared not rest or light the fires they so desperately needed. But fires of hate burned in their hearts. For Black Kettle's people, the cold darkness surrounding them seemed eternal. Each step of their journey north ignited another reason to smoke the ceremonial pipe . . . the occasion would be war.

The majority of Black Kettle's band thought only of war now. War followed every step of their way to the South Fork of the Smoky Hill River, until they encountered outriders from the Cheyenne camp they sought, near a place called Bunch of Timbers. They rushed food out to feed Black Kettle's people. They had not eaten in almost three days. As they filled their empty stomachs, wood was thrown on the lodge fires to warm the frozen refugees. As the shock of their ordeal subsided the Cheyenne vented their anger and frustrations against their own leaders. They blamed Black Kettle for the massacre. Around the council fires his people howled him down and they removed Black Kettle as chief of their clan. They elected Leg-in-the-Water in his place. Over time they realized his striving for peace and believing the white man were his only sins. Within six weeks, Black Kettle again was chief of his people.

After a few days of rest and recuperation, the Cheyenne moved northeastward to the Solomon River in present-day Kansas where the Sioux were encamped. From there, runners were sent across the Great Plains to other tribes of Sioux, Cheyenne and Arapaho. Their message: assemble in council and talk of war against the whites. Before the council met, however, George Bent chose to return to his father's ranch. His wounds were painful and his trip from the Cheyenne camp was tortuous. With the help of his brother-in-law, Edmond Guerrier, Bent finally found rest and much needed medical attention in the comfort of his father's home.

Robert and his half brother, Charlie, reached the ranch a few days prior to George's arrival. After a few days shelter in the family home and much discussion, George decided to return to his mother's people, the Cheyenne. He took with him his half brother Charlie, his sister Julia and his step-mother, Yellow Woman. During their brief stay at their father's ranch, George and Charlie informed the elder Bent they had renounced their white heritage after nearly being murdered by his race. Little White Man listened patiently to his sons, frightened and saddened at Charlie's unbelievable change.

Only a few years ago, this youngest Bent exhibited the curiosity and laughter of a child. What stood before William Bent now was a fifteen-year-old warrior. His brown eyes now simmered in dark brooding pools of hatred. Anger and a thirst for revenge replaced the laughter of his childhood. And his voracious need became a holy quest. He never again returned to the Bent ranch as a son, although he once returned in an attempt to kill his father. William also saw the anger in George's eyes. Furthermore, he observed confusion, frustration and hatred for the deeds men do, but he did not see the same venom consuming Charlie.

By morning's end, only Mary and Robert Bent chose to remain in their father's world. In her sorrow and anger, Yellow Woman vowed never again to live in the white world. Julia had already married Edmond Guerrier[83] and chose to live with him and the Cheyenne. The dawn witnessed the last vestige of the Bent family, their final communion grown from Sand Creek's carnage. Little White Man experienced a loneliness he'd not felt since Owl Woman's death. Not only had this incident taken his family from him, but the West and the nation had irreparably lost peace with the Indian nations of Sioux, Cheyenne, and Arapaho. Its reverberation would culminate twelve years later near another river named the "Little Big Horn."

A few days before George and Charlie Bent returned to the Cheyenne and Sioux camp on the Smoky Hill River, Chivington, like Caesar leading his Roman legions, triumphantly marched his troops into Denver. Throngs of the "Queen City's" citizens welcomed the Third Colorado Volunteers as they displayed their profane trophies of scalps, body parts and new "tobacco pouches."

News of their "victory" at Sand Creek spread faster than rumors of gold strikes in mining camps throughout Colorado. This event found the *Miner's Register* in Central City advocating poisoning

---

[83]Edmond Guerrier was the son of William Guerrier and a Cheyenne woman. He was a trader and scout, but after Sand Creek, rode with George Bent as a Cheyenne warrior. Guerrier surrendered with the rest of the warring factions of the Cheyenne and Arapahoe in 1875 and settled on the Cheyenne reservations in Oklahoma. He eventually changed his name to "Ed Geary," after whom the town Geary, Oklahoma, is named.

all Indians, as had been done in one incident in Minnesota. There, immigrants saturated two or three boxes of bread with strychnine and "left the food on the road for the Indians to find . . . One hundred men, women and children died from the effects of the poison." The article continued "that is the kind of warfare we approve of, and should be glad to see it introduced here. It is cheaper pecuniarily than to kill them with powder and lead."

But not all who were present at Sand Creek exalted in Chivington's so called "victory." In a letter to his mother, Captain Silas Soule wrote:

> We have had considerable trouble with the Indians this fall. The day you wrote, I was present at a massacre of three hundred Indians, mostly women and children. It was a horrible scene and I would not let my company fire. They were friendly and some of our soldiers were in their camp at the time, trading. It looked too hard for me to see little children on their knees begging for their lives have their brains beat out like dogs. It was a regiment of 100 days men who accomplished the noble deed.[84]

Soule's letter was uncommon. For in "the year of our Lord, 1864," the "Queen City" desecrated Christmas as its citizens blasphemed "peace on earth and good will towards men." On December 22nd *The Rocky Mountain News* reported, "Cheyenne scalps are getting as thick here as toads in Egypt. Everybody has got one, and is anxious to get another to send east." The next day, the *News* stated, "streets, hotels, saloons and stores were thronged with strangers, chiefly the 'Indian killers.' A high old time there was last night, around!"

On Christmas Eve the paper stated a raffle was held for a Navajo blanket found "on a defunct Indian at the Battle of Sand Creek." And on the night of December 28, 1864, the Denver Theatre treated, a "very full and fashionable audience" to a special play. The *News* further reported, it "was put upon the stage in splendid style, with numerous novel trappings, trophies of the big fight at Sand Creek. The piece will be repeated this evening, when everyone ought to see it for themselves." Among the "trappings" was a rope of 100 Indian scalps.

Chivington must have thought his triumph would impress the governor and eastern military establishments. In his much inflated

---

[84]Unpublished letter from Silas Soule to his mother, December 18, 1864.

report, Chivington stated he had killed over 500 warriors, including Cheyenne chiefs Black Kettle (who was very much alive at the time), White Antelope, Old Yellow Wolf and One-Eye. He also reported his men killed the Arapaho chief, Left Hand. However, Left Hand survived and lived to be an old man. Chivington's report failed to mention his men slaughtered mostly women, children and old men. He was not the only one to "exaggerate" the incident at Sand Creek.

Colonel George Shoup, Chivington's second in command wrote to a friend on December 3, 1864, saying,

> I have the pleasure of informing you, that we engaged the Indians on yesterday about forty miles North of Fort Lyon. The engagement commenced at sunrise, and lasted until about 2½ o'clock, completely routing the Indians.
>
> Our loss is (8) eight killed, one missing and about forty wounded. The Indian loss is variously estimated from 300 to 500, I think about 300..I think this is the severest chastisement ever given to Indians in battle on the American Continent.
>
> Our men fought with great enthusiasm and bravery, but with some disorder . . . I fear, however, they (the Indians) will loose (sic) their assumed bravery, when they hear of the defeat of their allies in arms. The story of that Indians are equals in warfare is nailed.

Within a month, the Cheyenne, Arapaho and Sioux disproved Shoup's words and continued to do so for the next twelve years.

In a letter to his brother, Major Scott Anthony not only lied about the battle, but he also lied about the execution style murder of young Jack Smith. Anthony stated, "We, of course, took no prisoners, except John Smith's son, and he was taken suddenly ill in the night and died before morning."

Chivington's reported deeds pleased many of Denver's citizens but it infuriated Edward "Tall Chief" Wynkoop. Wynkoop publicly denounced his superior officer as a liar and a murderer and sent telegrams to Congress and the President of the United States demanding an investigation into this deplorable act of violence against peaceful Cheyenne and Arapahos. Wynkoop's actions cost him his military career, but he vowed to fight for a people he knew to be honorable.

Word of their slaughter spread throughout the western plains by messengers on fast Indian ponies, who raced out to villages of Sioux, Cheyenne, and Arapaho. And their message was war. While

Indian ponies rode the plains, telegraph wires sang across the white world and spread word of Chivington's carnage.

As those couriers raced across the plains and wire, George and Charlie Bent arrived at a Cheyenne camp on Cherry Creek. Their familiarity with the village seemed strange now, because mourning for the dead still prevailed. And beneath the anguished cries of women, the Bents heard uncommon talk of winter war. The pipes had been sent out, first to the Sioux on the Solomon River, then to the Northern Arapaho, Cheyenne Dog soldiers, Spotted Trail's Sioux and Pawnee Killer's Sioux. When word of Sand Creek reached the Northern Cheyenne and Sioux, their pipes smoldered, and its smoke trail drifted to a small band of Oglala Sioux. Their leader Curley traveled south to join this fight. Within five years, his obscurity as a war leader would vanish like the ghost of Custer's fight. Almost twelve years later, at a river called Little Big Horn, he would be known forevermore to history as Crazy Horse.

All of these tribes moved their lodges and camps to meet the Southern Cheyenne on Cherry Creek. In the winter of 1864-1865, the peoples of Cheyenne, Sioux and Arapaho nations declared war on the United States. These tribes had never attempted a major winter war before. Then again, the Cheyenne and Arapaho had never before witnessed the kind of butchery their people endured at Sand Creek.

In a time of year the Cheyenne called the "Moon of the Strong Cold" (January), the assembled council decided to attack the northeastern Colorado town of Julesburg. Criers rode throughout the camps to tell of the chiefs' decision. For the first time in history, over one thousand warriors from the Sioux, Cheyenne and Arapaho nations gathered to make war against the whites. It was an incredible sight for George Bent. He watched as feathered war shields and bonnets, lances and rifles filled the camp. As the men readied for battle, George observed the women who accompanied this force. They brought extra horses to carry back what plunder they expected to find. As this vast column marched out of camp, the soldier societies overshadowed the younger braves, so none would slip off to accidentally or foolishly warn the town of Julesburg of their presence. According to custom, those who smoked the pipes first were given the honor of leading the column. Sioux chiefs led the largest of all war parties. One month and three days after barely surviving the massacre at Sand Creek, George and Charlie Bent painted themselves for war, as did one woman named Mochi!

In 1865, the town of Julesburg, located about 200 miles north-east of Denver near the Nebraska border was a stage stop. It sat one mile east of Lodgepole Creek's mouth on the south side of the South Platte River. The town consisted of a large "company" house, an eating house, a blacksmith and repair shop, a big stable, a corral, a large granary and store houses. Near the center of this small town stood a large store which sold goods to travelers and immigrants on the Overland Stage line and Platte River Trail. The forty to fifty station hands, stock tenders, drivers and telegraph operators living there, were lodged in buildings constructed of cottonwood logs and sod. Besides being a way station, Julesburg also served as an army camp. Camp Rankin, garrisoned by one company of the Seventh Iowa Cavalry was erected from the same type of buildings and surrounded its perimeters with a sod wall stockade. The town and fort was in fact an island of people, horses, sod and logs on a sea of plains below towering bluffs. Unbeknownst to its citizens, they were about to be surrounded by a torrent of angry Sioux, Cheyenne and Arapaho warriors!

The Sioux, Cheyenne and Arapaho didn't seem to mind January's cold, as they camped in the sand hills just south of Julesburg. Winter's breath could not be felt beneath their buffalo robes and blankets, as they settled in for the night. But the anticipation of the next morning's fight gave them little sleep. The cold Colorado wind followed warrior societies' every move in their constant vigil for exuberant young warriors seeking to count first coup.

At Camp Rankin and in Julesburg itself, life went on as normal as the people awakened. They were unaware of the imminent changes awaiting them on the morning of January 7th. As the curtain of dawn unfolded, it revealed over one thousand Indian warriors laying in wait in the ravines southeast of Camp Rankin.

Big Crow, a Cheyenne chief of the Crooked Lance Society, received the honor of drawing Camp Rankin's soldiers out into the open. His plan was an old, effective one. Big Crow and ten warriors, acting as decoys, hoped to lure the soldiers into chasing them. If they succeeded, the Cheyenne would lead them to the main body of Indians hidden in the ravines. There, the Indians would kill them all in one big ambush.

At first light, Big Crow and his warriors noticed a group of soldiers milling around outside Camp Rankin's stockade. With screams, yells and gunshots, Big Crow and his men rode out of the gully and charged the soldiers. Meanwhile, lookouts from the main body of Sioux, Cheyenne and Arapaho rode throughout camp and readied everyone for the attack.

The soldiers outside the stockade ran for the fort's protection as the bugler sounded the alarm. Within minutes, sixty soldiers rode from the stockade in pursuit of Big Crow's party. Their plan almost worked. As the cavalry gained on the decoys, young warriors hidden in the ravines could no longer be contained. Their anger and the excitement of the impending fight unharnessed their passion for revenge. They attacked before the soldiers were near enough to close off their escape.

When Captain Nicholas J. O'Brien saw the swarms of Sioux and Cheyenne pouring out of the ravines, he immediately wheeled his troops around. But it was too late for some of his men. Big Crow turned his decoys around and charged the troops. Starving Elk, another Cheyenne Chief, killed the bugler. The few cavalrymen who jumped from their horses to fight on foot were surrounded and killed. The main body of Sioux, Cheyenne and Arapaho attacked the fleeing soldiers on all sides, but were unable to cut off their escape into the stockade.

Almost simultaneously as the town and fort were attacked, the westbound stage driver arrived with his passenger, the Army paymaster. Just as the Indians ambushed Captain O'Brien's men, the driver whipped his team of horses, racing them on to the station as fast as they could run. As he arrived, he threw down his line and jumped off his box. The driver, the paymaster and the station hands all scrambled as fast as they could for the fort's safety and arrived at its gates the same time as Captain O'Brien's troops. Fourteen soldiers of the Seventh Iowa and four civilians died on the first day of the Indian war.

Because their surprise failed to kill all of the soldiers, the Indians broke off their attack on the fort. They had no desire to charge trained marksmen inside a fortified breastwork. Instead, they circled the stockade and rode to the stage station. The women with the extra ponies rode down to Julesburg as the Sioux, Cheyenne and Arapaho plundered the station. Inside, George Bent sat down at the table where breakfast had been served to the station hands only moments before. He and several Indians ate a hearty meal before they started looting the town. Bent saw one old warrior take a fancy to a big sugar bowl,

> He tied it to his belt. I saw him afterward riding off with
> the big bowl dangling from his belt behind him. The Indians

took whatever they wanted, but did not touch the canned goods, as they did not know what they were. The big warehouse belonging to the stage company was also plundered. From it the Indians secured all the flour, bacon, corn and sugar their ponies could carry. Some of the warriors found a big tin box and knocked the lock off. It was full of pieces of green paper. The Indians handled the paper but did not know what it was. One man took a big bundle of paper, chopped it into three or four pieces with his tomahawk, and threw it up in the air, laughing as the wind blew the fragments across the valley. I came up and secured a good deal of the money, but the Indians had already nearly emptied the paymaster's box. They threw the bills away . . . The soldiers later had a fine paper hunt and picked up money all over the prairie.

Nearly all day the Indians kept up the plunder, taking load after load of goods and provisions into the hills. The soldiers did not interfere and could not even come out to pick up the dead bodies of their comrades. At the station I found an express package addressed to some officer in Colorado, and in the package was a new major's uniform. I took it and later wore it during the fighting on Powder River when we fought General (P.E.) Connor's troops.[85]

Many Indians wanted to torch the buildings and fort, but the chiefs stopped them. They said they might want to return another day for more provisions. This day, the Indians spared the town and fort. The Cheyenne and Charlie Bent, on the 7th of January, experienced a turning point. Charlie, the youngest Bent brother savored his first taste of blood and he desired more.

With their pouches overflowing with plunder, it took the Cheyenne, Sioux and Arapaho three days to return to their camps on Cherry Creek. They returned to the village in triumph and for the first time since Sand Creek, no mourning for their dead was heard. A blow had been struck in revenge. Young men and women held scalp dances in the camps celebrating the deaths of soldiers and civilians killed at Julesburg. They danced and drummed until well after daylight. For days they celebrated and feasted on the white men's food they looted. The Cheyenne tomahawk became a can opener for the canned goods George Bent plundered from the stores. Their weapons opened beef, bacon, flour, corn meal, shelled corn, sugar and molasses. These nomads of the plains relished many of these foods for the first time.

---

[85] *The Life of George Bent*, pp. 172–173.

During this celebration, the chiefs held council. They decided to travel north to the Black Hills and Powder River area to ask the Northern Cheyenne and Sioux to join their massive war on the white man.

Small war parties attacked along the Platte River, above and below Julesburg, without looting for goods. These parties, along with Charlie Bent, struck at whites with vengeance, inflaming winter's land into the fires of Hell. In Kansas, Nebraska, and eastern Colorado, they burned stage stations, and telegraph poles, and attacked ranches, wagon trains, and small settlements. White women were forced to watch their husbands, fathers and brothers being murdered. They were then raped and taken captive to Indian camps.

One eyewitness reported seeing Charlie Bent leading a group of Cheyenne Dog Soldiers against Downer's stage station on the Smoky Hill road. Eight whites escaped the initial attack by hiding in a nearby cave, but Bent eventually lured them out with a promise not to harm them. When they emerged from the cave's shelter, the witness said, Charlie opened fire, killing one man and wounding five others. According to the witness, the two others were not as fortunate — they were captured.

After the Dog Soldiers pillaged and burned the station, they turned their attention to the prisoners. As five others escaped and watched, Bent staked one of the now naked captives spread-eagle on the ground. Bent then cut out the man's tongue and replaced it with "another portion" of the man's body. Little White Man's youngest son then started a fire on the captive's stomach. The captive's screams of agony were drowned out by Bent's and the other Dog Soldiers' howls of ecstasy. These men died slow, horrible deaths at the hands of a young madman. Upon hearing of Charlie's atrocities, William Bent disowned his youngest son. And even though George Bent continued to live and fight with the Cheyenne, he too could not condone Charlie's actions. Soon afterwards he cut his ties with his half brother.

Within three weeks of their first attack, the Cheyenne and Sioux again sacked the town of Julesburg and almost every white rancher, farmer and settler in eastern Colorado, western Kansas and Nebraska was killed or attacked. William Bent's fears of what could happen became a reality. In the waning days of the Civil War, President Abraham Lincoln ordered 8,000 troops away from those bloody battlefields to fight a new Indian war. He sent troops to the frontiers of Colorado, Wyoming, Kansas and Nebraska and, eventually, to the Dakotas and Montana.

"Ned" Wynkoop's reports to Washington did not fall on deaf ears and, ironically, the day Congress announced a full investigation of Sand Creek, the Colorado Third Volunteer Cavalry was mustered out of the Army. Their hundred day enlistment was over, and within a few days, Colonel John Chivington resigned his commission and left the Army!

10
Hearings, Heresy and Homicide

Truth is often hidden in many ways
And not all beliefs are true.
When lies have been spoken for many days
Reality is hard to construe.

Two gunshots pierced the pleasant April night, momentarily silencing the throng on Denver's streets. For Silas Soule's bride of three weeks, the silence was deafening. When the city's pathways again filled with people, they shouted and ran towards the gunshot's source. There they discovered the body of a young man lying dead on a dust covered walkway with a bullet in his brain. Ironically, Captain Silas Soule had predicted his own murder. And his untimely death gave birth to untold stories and legends in Colorado's history.

Where there are legends, there are heroes who are often born from tragedy, and the embryo from which they are conceived is adversity. In the twenty-six years of his life, Silas Soule's essence had been nourished by the milk of valor. Those who knew him understood that injustice and prejudice were aberrations to his soul and he feared neither death nor the threat of it in his quest to fight these vexations to mankind's existence. In the tradition of ancient heroes, Soule began his adventures long before he was a man.

Six years before the Civil War, Missouri border gangs ravaged the Kansas-Missouri border with murder, robbery, and arson. Their goal was to create a pro-slavery state of Kansas, while equally determined abolitionists sought to keep Kansas "a homestead of the free." Murder begat murder and soon raiders on both sides vehemently sought vengeance in bloody prelude to civil war.

The clash between these two factions struck like a bolt of lightning during the spring of 1856. On May 21, a group of Missouri raiders sacked and burned Lawrence, Kansas, which "Free Staters" considered their center. Although Missouri raiders killed only two people, the attack's consequences were grave. Three days later, a band of fanatical abolitionists led by John Brown found five pro-slavery settlers camped along the banks of Pottawatomie Creek. He and his men hacked them to pieces with artillery swords. That deed inflamed America's western frontier. Hatred, bloodshed and an obsession for vengeance were its aftermath.

Against this backdrop, fifteen year old Silas Soule ventured west with his father, Amasa, from Boston, one year before Brown's raid. In Kansas he became an active member of the "underground railroad." Armed with "Beecher's Bibles,"[86] Soule and other eastern abolitionists helped escaping slaves on their journey to freedom. They rode as "jayhawkers" throughout "bleeding" Kansas for almost five years. His prowess as a guerrilla raider showed in 1859, when Soule and four others rescued famed underground "railroader" Dr. John Doy. Doy's conviction and sentence to five years imprisonment for transporting runaway slaves to safety made it imperative for the abolitionists to act. The day before Doy's transfer to the Missouri State Prison, Soule's band broke into a St. Joseph jail and released him.

In the same year, after John Brown's capture at Harper's Ferry, Virginia, Soule became involved in a daring plan to break him out of prison. However, Soule's attempt never transpired and he returned to the West. Soule's adventures took him to the very hell holes of violence, yet he matured well beyond his nineteen years and somewhere amidst the gun smoke and dust of the Kansas frontier, he lost his youth.

From the Kansas plains to Colorado's gold fields, Soule rode into manhood and history on a stallion called "Destiny." Within a

---

[86]Beecher's Bibles were rifles that were paid for and shipped to the abolitionists with the blessings of the famous Brooklyn clergyman Henry Ward Beecher. Beecher's sister was Harriet Beecher Stowe, whose book *Uncle Tom's Cabin* helped ignite the debate on slavery in the United States.

Captain Silas Soule.   Photo courtesy Colorado Historic Society

span of a single turbulent decade, that mystical "steed" who guides all men, took him to Sand Creek on the 29th day of November, 1864, to witness one of America's greatest tragedies. Only Soule and a handful of officers, out of 700 soldiers present, dared confront the man responsible — Colonel John Chivington. Soule's meeting with Chivington wasn't his first — nor his last.

These two men had met each other four years before in 1860. Two years later both participated in the Battle of Glorieta Pass. The young "jayhawker," then a lieutenant, served under then Major Chivington of the First Colorado Regiment. Both men fought valiantly and earned reputations as being fearless, but these two men held no fondness for each other. Chivington often used his massive size to intimidate those who disagreed with him, but Soule demonstrated time and again he held no fear of the former preacher's bulk. The young captain defied Chivington on numerous occasions. Ironically, the former man of God's ability to forgive his enemies or to turn the other cheek did not exist. Soule and Chivington clashed one last, fatal time after Sand Creek. It began with a newspaper banner.

On December 30, 1864, the *Rocky Mountain News* carried the headline "'High Officials' Spur Investigation." The paper recounted "Ned" Wynkoop's reports to Washington, D.C. This infuriated not only Washington officials, but almost the entire population of Denver. They directed their rage, not towards Chivington and his troops, but towards "High Officials" and Major Wynkoop! The same issue of the *News* reiterated the fabled reports and letters Chivington, Shoup and Anthony had written. The paper questioned "who those 'high officials' were;" while many of the "Bloody Third" and their admirers stated with more than mild intimation "that they had half a mind to 'go for them.' Threats spread throughout the city of stringing up those betraying the 'boys of the Third.'"

In the following weeks, while the Queen City waited, officials were already in Denver and at Fort Lyon taking affidavits from those who had witnessed the "incident" at Sand Creek. To the dismay of "Bloody Third" members, an investigation had indeed begun and officials were questioning people about what they had seen and heard. They suspected most of these men, including their leader Colonel Chivington, were glad they had mustered out of the army!

Two of the complainants were Major Edward Wynkoop and Captain Silas Soule, but the "high official" turned out to be

Colorado's Chief Justice Benjamin Hall. Others complaining to Washington were Indian agent Samuel Colley and Lt. Colonel Samuel Tappan.

On January 8, 1865, from his wintry isolated post at Fort Lyon, Soule wrote home to his mother,

> I hope the authorities at Washington will investigate the killings of these Indians. I think they will be apt to hoist some of our high officials. I would not fire on the Indians with my Company and the Colonel said he would have me cashiered, but he is out of the service before me and I think that I stand better than he does in regard to his great Indian fight.[87]

The day before he wrote this letter, the combined forces of the Sioux, Cheyenne and Arapaho sacked Julesburg, Colorado.

In Washington, D.C., two days after Soule wrote home, the House of Representatives passed the motion:

> that the Committee on the Conduct of the War be required to inquire into and report all the facts connected with the late attack of the third regiment of Colorado volunteers, under Colonel Chivington, on the Cheyenne tribe of Indians, near Fort Lyon.[88]

The inquiry's immediate action shocked those awaiting word of the investigation. It relieved some but outraged others.

Within less than two weeks of Soule's letter to his mother, the Army appointed him Provost Marshall of the district and transferred him to Denver. Five weeks later, he testified against Chivington in a military investigation.

As the investigation began to unveil, the frontier citizens of Denver split themselves into two camps — pro-Chivington or pro-Wynkoop and Soule. Those same citizens liked Wynkoop and Soule, especially Soule, because of his jovial, devil-may-care personality. But even folks who thought well of these men treated their charges against Chivington as something akin to heresy. Many in town looked upon the huge former preacher as a man larger than life. Wasn't he the man who helped bring God's word to the godless during Denver's infancy? And wasn't he the hero of Glorieta Pass? Wasn't it Chivington who promised protection for Colorado's citizens against slavery's sins and hostile attacks from "savages"?

Why would two brother officers do this to a man they had known and fought beside for years? Were they jealous of his victory

[87]Unpublished letter of Silas Soule, January 8, 1865.
[88]"Massacre of Cheyenne Indians," p. 3.

over "500" Cheyenne and Arapaho warriors? Or were some of the other stories whispered in town really true, that maybe there were mostly women and children in the village at Sand Creek?

Soon those whispers were spoken aloud, then written down with pen and ink. In fact whispers became sworn statements. In his affidavit taken at Fort Lyon, John Smith gave a detailed account of his service as an interpreter and trader. In reference to Chivington's attack at Sand Creek, Smith, the man who probably knew the Cheyenne better than any white man alive save William Bent, stated,

> When the troops first approached, I endeavoured to join them, but we was repeatedly fired upon, as also the soldier and the civilian with me.
>
> When the troops began approaching, I saw Black Kettle, the head chief, hoist the American flag over his lodge, as well as a white flag, fearing there might be some mistake as to who they were . . .[89]

Lieutenant James D. Cannon, of the first New Mexico volunteer infantry, after being duly sworn, said,

> In going over the battle ground the next day, I did not see a body of a man, woman or child but was scalped; and in many instances their bodies were mutilated in the most horrible manner, men, women, and children-privates cut out, etc. I heard one man say that he had cut a woman's private parts out, and had them for exhibition on a stick; I heard another man say that he had cut off the fingers of an Indian to get the rings off the hand. According to the best of my knowledge and belief, these atrocities that were committed were with the knowledge of J. M. Chivington, and I do not know of his taking any measure to prevent them . . .[90]

Some of the evidence, however, was self-explanatory. Didn't Colonel Shoup write the Cheyenne would lose their will to fight after the defeat of their warriors? Why then had the Indian war increased a hundred fold since Sand Creek? Some stories simply did not make sense to those who listened with logic. But those deafened by their hatred for Indians chose to believe Chivington's version of Sand Creek.

From March 13 through March 15, 1865, a Congressional Committee on the Conduct of War held its first hearings. The

---

[89]"Massacre of Cheyenne Indians," p. 5
[90]The Chivington Massacre, Affidavit, January 16, 1865, p. 53.

committee called Governor John Evans, who was already in Washington, to testify first. As Territorial Governor, Evans was Superintendent of Indian affairs. Through his testimony, he convinced Congress of one thing — he possessed no knowledge of plains Indians or their customs. Time and again, when asked about Cheyenne hierarchy, he answered with confusion and contradiction. When the Committee on the Conduct of War asked Evans, "Have you any knowledge of any acts committed by either of those chiefs (Black Kettle and White Antelope), or by the bands immediately under their control-any personal knowledge?"

Evans' answer was cut short when he stated, "In 1862, a party of these Dog Soldiers . . ."

The Committee interrupted Evans by stating, "I am not asking about the Dog Soldiers, but about Black Kettle's band."

Evans shot back, "They are the same Indians. The Dog Soldiers were a sort of vigilance committee under those old chiefs."

The Committee then reminded Evans, "I understood you to say, a few minutes ago that the Dog Soldiers threw off the authority of the old chiefs, and were independent of them."

One of the last questions the Committee asked the Governor was, "With all the knowledge you have in relation to these attacks and depredations by the Indians, do you think they afford any justification for the attack made by Colonel Chivington on these friendly Indians, under the circumstances under which it was made?"

The ever political Evans' answer was non-committal.

> As a matter of course, no one could justify an attack on Indians while under the protection of the flag. If those Indians were under the protection of the flag, it would be a question that would be scarcely worth asking, because nobody could say anything in favor of the attack. I have heard, however — that is only a report — that there was a statement on the part of Colonel Chivington and his friends that these Indians had assumed a hostile attitude before he attacked them. I do not know whether that is so or not. I have said all I have to do with them. I suppose they were being treated as prisoners of war in some way or other."[91]

Meanwhile, one month before Denver's Congressional hearings commenced[92] the Secretary of War appointed military officials to

---

[91]"Massacre of Cheyenne Indians," p. 38.
[92]Congressional hearings were being held in Denver and Washington, D.C., during the same time period.

investigate the massacre. The commission appointed Lt. Colonel Samuel Tappan as its chair. Chivington, infuriated by this appointment, appealed to the board, stating,

> Gentlemen: I would most respectfully object to Lieutenant Colonel S.F. Tappan, first veteran battalion Colorado cavalry, being a member of the commission, for the following reasons to wit:
>
> 1st: That the said Lieutenant Colonel S.F. Tappan is and for a long time past has been, my open and avowed enemy.
>
> 2nd. That the said Lieutenant Colonel S.F. Tappan has repeatedly expressed himself very much prejudiced against the killing of the Indians near Fort Lyon, Colorado Territory, commonly known as the battle of 'Sand Creek,' and has said that it was a disgrace to every officer connected with it, and that he (Tappan) would make it appear so in the end.
>
> 3rd. That I believe, from a full knowledge of his character, that he cannot divest himself of his prejudices sufficiently to render an impartial verdict, and is, therefore, not such a judge as the law contemplates when it directs that all men shall be tried by an impartial tribunal.[93]

Chivington's objections were overruled after Tappan clarified his statements and his feelings on Chivington's actions.

The hearings proceeded on February 15, 1865. The first witness called to testify was Captain Silas Soule. Prior to his testimony, Soule received numerous death threats. True to his nature though, he was not intimidated. As a result of these threats, he determined to fulfill his duty as an officer; the truth would be known one way or the other. On his opening testimony to the Commission, Soule calmly answered questions about his name, age, rank, time in service and the events leading up to Sand Creek. He included his meeting with Chivington and his troops, two days before the massacre. The Commission then adjourned until 9:30 A.M. the next day.

February 16 was the seventh day of the hearing, but only the second day of testimony. For the very first time, the truth was being told, under oath, about the actual events that took place on November 29, 1864. For two and a half days, the Commission questioned Soule in minute detail about the events he witnessed at Sand Creek. They also queried his observations on his return trip to the massacre site.

---

[93] "The Sand Creek Massacre," p. 5.

During those days, the massive Chivington glared at Soule and took notes. Then, on the 17th of February at 2:00 P.M., Chivington took his turn to ask questions. Chivington, who gave no quarter at Sand Creek, showed no mercy during his cross examination of Soule. The former Colonel relentlessly probed Soule's testimony for any inconsistencies. Unshaken, the young Captain again showed his nemesis he would not be bullied and survived Chivington's three days of torturous questioning. Lt. Crammer and Major Wynkoop both supported Soule's testimony, as did Old Jim Beckwourth, who had acted as a scout during the massacre.

For some reason, Chivington feared Beckwourth's testimony as much as he did Soule's. As the Commission began swearing in the old great mountain man, Chivington objected! The former preacher tried to disqualify Beckwourth. To the Commission's surprise as well as to the surprise of everyone present, Chivington asked that the witness, James P. Beckwourth "be interrogated as to his belief in the existence of God, who rewards good and punishes evil, before he is sworn."[94] Chivington knew Beckwourth had lived among various western tribes for over forty years and was a Crow war chief. The possibility of Chivington impeaching this witness before he uttered a single word was great if Beckwourth confessed to being heathen.

When asked by the Commission, "Do you believe in the existence of a Supreme Being, of a God, by whom truth is enjoined and falsehood punished, and do you consider the form of administering an oath as binding upon your conscience?" The sixty-nine year old, Beckwourth simply answered, "I do." From his almost fifty years of living with the Indians, Beckwourth knew their beliefs in the great spirits of the sky, earth and winds were generally much more reverent and less hypocritical than those beliefs of many whites, especially a man like Chivington. Beckwourth probably got a chuckle this so-called man of God was under investigation for ordering the mass slaughter of peaceful old men, women and children.

Age had not diminished Beckwourth's mind and he was still as strong as a bull, although he had only slightly more than a year and a half to live after his testimony. Chivington challenged Beckwourth's statements to the Commission time and again, not because of their content, but because of the old mountain man's origin, race and religion and his relationship with the Indians of whom he spoke.

---

[94]Ibid., p. 68.

However, many commission members and even Chivington himself were fully acquainted with Beckwourth's background.

Although a proud and eloquent speaker, James Pierson Beckwourth was born a slave in Frederick County, Virginia, around 1796. His father, a Virginia aristocrat, Sir Jennings Beckwith,[95] had an affair with one of his slaves, known only as "Miss Kill." To the total horror of Frederick County's aristocracy, Jennings Beckwith, whose English ancestry could be traced as far back as the Battle of Hastings, actually married the girl. The scandal created by this marriage in 1810 forced Beckwith to relocate to the wilderness area around Saint Louis, Missouri. His father educated young Jim as he grew up. Though laws prohibited it, Jennings nonetheless taught his son to read and write and at the age of fourteen, Jim began an apprenticeship to a blacksmith. The call of the wild, though, soon lured Jim to the west, to the plains and mountains beyond. Before he left home, his father emancipated him and young Beckwourth set forth to become one of America's greatest mountain men. Fifty years later, because of Chivington's personal feelings toward men of "color," he attempted his best legal maneuvers to discredit Beckwourth by assailing his character.

In one instance of Beckwourth's testimony, Chivington objected to a conversation the old man had had with a Cheyenne chief named Leg-in-the-Water on the grounds, "The statements of Indians are never received as evidence even when the Indians are personally present, except in cases where it is specially authorized by statute."[96] The Commission overruled the objection.

When the Commission asked Beckwourth about Cheyenne and Arapahoe treatment of children and women taken in battle from their enemies, Chivington raised another objection. Again he was overruled. The Commission allowed Old Jim his answer. "The children are treated kindly; the women are generally violated"[97]

However, Beckwourth was not allowed to answer the final question the Commission asked, "Do they (the Cheyenne and Arapaho) often kill, scalp and otherwise mutilate women or children taken prisoners by them in battle?"[98] Chivington's

---

[95]Jim's name changes from Beckwith to Beckwourth throughout Wyoming, Colorado and Montana. Most biographers use the name Beckwourth, which, in later years, was how the great mountain man himself spelled it.
[96]Ibid., p. 72.
[97]"The Sand Creek Massacre," p. 74.
[98]Ibid., p. 74.

booming voice sounded an objection the Commission finally sustained.

Jim Beckwourth spoke well and truthfully in his testimony. Chivington's probing and gruelling questioning failed to intimidate the old man. Though he tried, Chivington could find no holes in his story. The former Colonel's contempt for Beckwourth's color only made his failure to challenge the mountain man's testimony more demeaning.

The hearing into the Sand Creek Massacre lasted a total of seventy-six days. Those hearings saw Chivington bring in dozens of witnesses who had been members of the "Bloody Third" and whose testimony all sounded the same, Indians dug rifle pits or they were dressed up as "squaws."

Stephen Decatur, formerly a sergeant of the Third Colorado Regiment, stated,

> The next day after the battle I went over to the battle-ground, in the capacity of clerk, for Lieutenant Colonel Bowen, and counted four hundred and fifty dead Indian warriors . . . I saw, comparatively speaking, a small number of women killed.
>
> There were a great many of them (rifle pits), I did not count the number; they were deep enough for men to lie down and conceal themselves, and load their guns in; some of them I should think deeper than three feet.[99]

Throughout this bizarre period in Denver's history, tempers flared and fights erupted in the streets between pro- and anti-Chivington camps. On two separate occasions, attempts were made on Silas Soule's life, whose job it was to keep the peace. Although Soule had finished his testimony against Chivington two weeks earlier, the hearings were still in full swing. Ned Wynkoop advised his friend to be careful while in the streets. He knew the "Chivington people" would exact a revenge on all who defamed their leader. Soule appreciated his warnings, but the young captain already knew he was going to die.

The very marrow of courage is selfless aggression. And valor's pinnacle is oftened reached through truth's sometime harsh eloquence. Within its annals, the cost of justice is often life itself. Soule treated his quest for justice as though it were for the Holy Grail itself. In the later part of March, Sile and his friend Captain George Price decided to take advantage of a beautiful spring day.

---

[99]Ibid., p. 195.

They hired a buggy and rode to Central City. They talked of many things, as young men do, including Sile's new found love, the daughter of rancher Charles Coberly. He asked his friend, George, to be the best man at his wedding. A more sombering conversation, though, replaced Soule's talk of love. He was also worried. He told Price of his overwhelming premonition of doom. He felt his testimony against Chivington would cost him his life. He was not frightened by the Grim Reaper's afterworld. What scared him existed in the Commission's hearings. He told Price he felt his "character would be assailed"[100] and an attempt to destroy his testimony would be made.

George told his friend and comrade from the war-torn plains of Colorado, if Soule's prediction came true, he would fight those persons questioning his character. The two young warriors made a pact: the truth about Sand Creek would be heard and documented for all time! Within thirty days of their talk, Silas Soule was dead!

Before his death however, Soule did experience love's ecstasy. He married and, as promised, his friend George Price stood up as his best man. It all ended on an April night three weeks later. The weather was surprisingly pleasant for that time of year. A slight breeze breathed its way into Denver on its journey from the plains. Only the cottonwood trees standing their lone vigil along the Platte River's banks felt its touch as it quietly entered the city. Most of Denver's good citizens were indoors, at home or visiting with friends.

That's how it was for Sile and his wife. Between 9:30 and 10:00 P.M. on the last night of his life, Soule and his new bride returned home to Curtis Street from visiting friends. After a short time inside, a number of

> shots were fired in the upper part of the city, evidently to decoy him out and the Captain started to ascertain the cause. While passing along Lawrence Street, near F, and directly in front of the residence of Dr. Cunningham, he seems to have been met by the assassin and the indications are that both men fired at the same instant . . .

Soule lay dead with a bullet in his brain. Evidence at the scene, though, indicated Soule had wounded his assassin. The killer dropped his gun and left a distinct blood trail that led away from the murder scene towards the military camp.

---

[100]Ibid., p. 189.

The city streets quickly filled with people and patrols were ordered out to find the Provost Marshall's killer. The murder of the likeable and capable Silas Soule shocked the entire town. John Walley, the city's undertaker, carried Soule's lifeless body with reverence to his mortuary. This solemn occasion would not be profaned by anyone.

Three days later, Soule's funeral services were held. His widow, friends and fellow officers attended and the church overflowed with mourners. Even Governor Evans came and paid his respects. Only Chivington and his followers were conspicuous in their absence. This break with military tradition was all the more debased the very next day, after the commission reconvened.

Chivington introduced an affidavit taken from a teamster named Lipman Meyer.[101] He read from a lengthy deposition taken at Fort Lyon that Meyer accused Captain Silas Soule of drunkenness in the line of duty, theft and cowardice. Upon hearing those ludicrous charges against his recently slain friend, Captain George Price angrily made an objection to the commission, saying the accusations in Meyer's deposition had nothing to do with the incident at Sand Creek. Price told the commission Meyer's deposition was nothing more than an attempt to blacken the name and reputation of a man who fought for his country! The young captain also reminded commission members Soule's only "sin" was courage, and it took a great deal of it to make a stand against injustices done to the Cheyenne and Arapaho people by Colonel John M. Chivington! George Price kept his pact with his friend, and Chivington's efforts to disqualify Silas Soule's testimony were in vain.

Over the vehement protests of Chivington, the commission agreed with Price's objection and Lipman Meyer's deposition was not received as evidence. As the hearings continued, the Cheyenne, Arapaho and Sioux waged their war against the whites. Their war, however, was not confined to Colorado alone.

The Southern Cheyenne's pilgrimage into Wyoming and South Dakota in the spring of 1865 went almost unnoticed. There, they banded together for the first time in almost forty years with their cousins, the Northern Cheyenne, and with tribes of the Sioux nation. It went unnoticed because of what was happening two thousand miles away in the East, in the land of the "Great White Father."

---

[101]Ibid., p. 189.

On April 9, 1865, Robert E. Lee surrendered to Ulysses S. Grant. It was Palm Sunday and the Union was again united. Five days later, John Wilkes Booth assassinated President Abraham Lincoln at Ford's Theatre in Washington, D.C. It was the first time in American history a President had been murdered. Within days of this tragedy, the army cornered Lincoln's killer in a Maryland barn and killed him. Lincoln's successor, Andrew Johnson, was a Southerner and rumored to be an alcoholic. The nation's democracy teetered on the very brink of anarchy.

Those resounding events in history muffled the gunshots piercing the pleasant night of April 23rd, when a young man was killed in the streets of Denver. But he was conceived again, through the tales of his deeds, into legend's netherland, like the ancient ones before him called "heroes."

11
Aftermath

Death begat death
In those western plains of old,
As the flames of war engulfed
Those months of wintry cold.

The Commission for the Conduct of War concluded its hearings on the seventy-sixth day of its existence. From February 9th through May 30th, 1865, the commission heard hundreds of hours of testimony and read affidavits from dozens of witnesses. Ulysses S. Grant, Commanding General of the Union Army, said that Chivington's actions amounted to nothing more than murder. And Joseph Holt, the Army's Judge Advocate General stated it was a "cowardly and cold blooded slaughter, sufficient to cover its perpetrators with indelible infamy and the face of every American with shame and indignation."[102]

When the hearings were over, it was obvious to the commission and others there had indeed been a tragic and brutal massacre of Cheyenne and Arapaho Indians at a place called "Sand Creek." It was also obvious no charges would ever be filed against any of the men responsible for this reprehensible crime against humanity, especially Shoup and Chivington. They were regarded too highly by men in prestigious places. Not even Silas Soule's killer was brought to justice.

---

[102] *The Indians*, p. 187.

A soldier named Squiers was Soule's accused killer. His wounds coincided with those inflicted by the Provost Marshall. Almost immediately after Soule's murder, Squiers deserted from the Colorado Second Infantry and fled to Las Vegas, New Mexico. While his search spread throughout Colorado, someone in New Mexico recognized him and sent a letter to Denver telling of his whereabouts. The army ordered First Lieutenant James D. Cannon to arrest him.

Cannon and a small detachment of men took the long arduous trail down to northern New Mexico. Once leaving Trinidad, Colorado, they rode to the summit of Raton Pass. Lined on either side by spruce- and pine-covered mountains the pass descends into New Mexico, where the "Land of Enchantment's" prairie desert comes into full view for hundreds of square miles.

When Cannon and his men arrived in Las Vegas, they promptly arrested Squiers without incident. The trooper offered no resistance, but hinted the lieutenant didn't know what he was getting into. Squiers' threats didn't bother Cannon. He too had been at Sand Creek and found the courage to testify against Chivington. It was Cannon's men of the New Mexico volunteers who helped save Charlie Bent from execution on the night of November 29th. To Cannon, men like Squiers were scum, and he strongly felt the army should divest itself of those types by use of rope or bullet.

When Cannon returned Squiers to Denver in mid-summer, it happened again. On July 14, 1865, authorities found twenty-four-year-old James D. Cannon dead in his Denver hotel room. And Squiers, who had been incarcerated in Denver's city jail, had disappeared! The suspected cause of Cannon's death was poison. He was the second officer murdered after testifying against Chivington and the others. The authorities never arrested anyone in connection with his death, and Squiers fled to California where he successfully eluded being brought to justice.

During these chaotic and violent months in 1865, the Cheyenne were still raiding eastern Colorado and Nebraska's and Kansas' western plains. The events formed on an almost dry river bed called Sand Creek, were now spilling over into Wyoming and the Dakotas.

Shortly after Julesburg had been sacked a second time, George Bent went north to the Powder River areas of South Dakota and Wyoming with the Cheyenne. There major skirmishes between the U.S. Army, the Sioux and Cheyenne became more frequent. In February of 1865, the Southern Cheyenne and Red Cloud's Oglala Sioux gathered in northwestern Nebraska and planned new raids against the army. It was in this massive camp that George Bent first looked upon his Northern Cheyenne cousins. The differences in appearance and language between those two tribes of the ancient Tsis Tsis Tas amazed him.

Bent remembered,

> These northern Kinsmen of ours were dressed very differently from us and looked strange to our eyes. Our southern Indians all wore cloth blankets, cloth leggings, and other things made by whites, but these northern Indians all wore buffalo robes and buckskin leggings; they had braided hair wrapped in strips of buckskin painted red, and they had crow feathers on their heads with the ends of the feathers cut off in a peculiar manner. They looked much wilder than any of the southern Indians, and kept up all the old customs, not having come in contact with the whites . . . They were growing more like the Sioux in habits and appearance every year.[103]

It had been almost forty years since these two tribes separated and twenty-two-year-old George Bent was too young to remember his Southern Cheyenne once looked like his Northern cousins.

During winter, the tribes moved their camps often to avoid detection. They moved again when spring made its way into this north land, this time to the basin of Wyoming's Big Horn Mountains. From there war parties started raiding the North Platte Road. The Cheyenne, Arapaho and Sioux attacked numerous stage stops and small army garrisons throughout the spring, including Camp Dodge, located about thirty miles south of present day Casper, Wyoming.

On July 25, over one thousand Sioux and Cheyenne attacked two troops of cavalry at Old Platte Bridge. The battle filled the hot, clear day with so much gunsmoke and dust that visibility was cut down to about a dozen yards. Few soldiers survived. One who did not was Lieutenant Caspar Collins.[104] During the thick of battle, he was shot in the forehead with an arrow. Shortly thereafter, the Wyoming Territory renamed Old Platte Bridge (and incorrectly spelled) Casper, in his honor.

---

[103] *The Life of George Bent*, p. 195.
[104] The Colorado city of Fort Collins was named in honor of Colonel William O. Collins, Caspar's father.

By now thousands of U.S. Troops were arriving from the Civil War's eastern battlefields to put down this new western Indian war. Up to this time, all efforts to quell the uprising had failed and western and eastern newspapers alike called for a change of tactics and command. The citizens demanded an experienced Indian fighter. More importantly, big businesses demanded help in clearing the west of Indians. Months earlier, the Overland Stage Company exerted its influential pressure on the War Department for an experienced Indian fighter. The result: Brigadier General P.E. Connor was sent east from his Utah command.

Patrick Edward (O') Connor was not a large man. Though he was small in stature, his reputation for getting things accomplished was huge. Born on Saint Patrick's day in 1820 in County Kerry, Ireland, he came to America as a young child. O'Connor's life in New York City's despised Irish-American section proved harsh and cruel. Within his five-foot six and one-half inch frame grew an ambition that took him from New York's poverty-laden streets to Stockton, California's gravel-covered streets — and to wealth beyond his dreams.

His escape from poverty came through the United States military. In November of 1839, nineteen-year-old O'Connor enlisted in the U.S. Army to fight the Seminole Indians. However, instead of combating mosquitoes, snakes and alligators of Florida's infamous Everglades in pursuit of the elusive Osceola, he found himself in the newly formed territory of Iowa. As a private, most of his duties were menial but physically demanding. In November of 1844, after five years of service, the Army honorably discharged him.

Two years later, after dropping the "O" from O' Connor and the "Patrick" from his formal name, P. Edward Connor enrolled as a first lieutenant in a three-month volunteer regiment to fight in the Mexican War. Here, he found himself in the midst of men who later became a veritable Who's Who of the great Civil War that followed fifteen years later: Albert Sidney Johnston, Braxton Bragg, Robert E. Lee and U.S. Grant. After being wounded in the battle of Buena Vista, Connor's reputation as a formidable fighter grew from his commendation for "conspicuous gallantry."

At the war's end, Connor moved west to Stockton, California, where he founded a prosperous gravel business. Discontented with peacetime's tedium, Connor kept his hand in local law enforcement and volunteer military service. When Mexican bandits terrorized northern California, it was Connor and his men who rode into action. Weeks later he and his "California Rangers" produced a bloody, severed head of a Mexican male and claimed it to be the "mythical" bandit, Joaquin Murieta. There were some rumors the head belonged to a luckless peon who was in the wrong place at the right time for Conner and his men. In the following eight years Connor became a wealthy man. When the Civil War erupted in 1861, Connor put his wealth aside and re-entered the service as a colonel in a California regiment.

Instead of going east of the Mississippi River, Connor and his troops were ordered into Utah and Nevada to quell the Shoshoni uprising. On January 29, 1863, on the banks of Utah's Bear River, he and his men surprised a large village and slaughtered 278 Indians, including many women and children. Through this carnage and his reputation as the man who got "Murieta," Connor emerged a hero of the western frontier.

Much to Chivington's dismay, who intensely disliked Connor, the general soon became popular in Colorado and Nebraska. Even though Chivington's popularity remained high in Colorado after the congressional hearings, he jealously guarded his fame as an Indian fighter and did not wish to share the limelight with anyone, particularly Conner. Chivington had not forgotten their clash just prior to Sand Creek, when he and Connor first met. The huge former colonel challenged the diminutive general's authority when the army ambiguously ordered Connor to take command of all troops between Salt Lake City and Fort Kearny, Nebraska. The order specified protection for the stage line against hostile Indians. When Connor tried to exert his "authority" over Chivington, he was not amazed at the colonel's defiance. Connor had heard tales about the former preacher and knew he held his position in Colorado's chain of command sacred. Ironically, it was Governor Evans, Chivington's friend and fellow Warren County, Ohio resident, who welcomed any military re-enforcements. However, by the time Connor took command and issued orders, Chivington had already commenced his march on Sand Creek. Politics, racial hatred and petty jealousies soon caused Chivington's fall from grace with military authorities.

Between April and May in 1865, the general ordered details of troops to protect the stage line. According to initial observations, the deployment of his troops seemed to have discouraged Indians raids. The army hadn't realized the Indians were still in winter camp. By mid-May, the tribes renewed their attacks on the roads with a boldness never before witnessed. The guerilla-style warfare of the Cheyenne, Arapaho and Sioux prevented Connor's stopping their raids. After they soundly defeated Collins' two troops of cavalry at Old Platte Bridge, the public began to panic. Had the Cheyenne and Sioux continued their raids through August, the roads probably would have been closed for years. Fortunately for whites, the Indians camped along the Powder River and held their ritual summer medicine ceremonies. Connor now had time to regroup. With his large force, he built a stockade near a favorite river crossing of the Sioux and Cheyenne. With his forces as well as a small army of Pawnee and Omaha Indian scouts, Connor implemented a change of tactics. While the general built his fort, the Pawnees watched for Cheyenne and Sioux.

The Indians set to their task well. On August 16, the Pawnee lured about thirty Cheyenne into one of their ambushes. George Bent's stepmother was among them. The Pawnee dressed themselves as Sioux and signaled the Cheyenne with their blankets. "We are friends; come nearer."[105] As the Cheyenne rode closer, they fell into the Pawnee's ambush. Five Cheyenne were killed. That night, the Pawnee scouts held a scalp dance at General Connor's camp. One among the freshly severed scalp locks they paraded on a stick as they sang belonged to Yellow Woman.

The war in the Wyoming plains was now escalating. A few days after Yellow Woman's death, Connor and his troops surprised a large Arapaho camp on Wolf Creek. His Pawnee and Omaha scouts raided their pony herd and a furious battle ensued. Although taken off guard, the infuriated Arapaho were able to turn Connor's forces back. The price they paid was high. The Arapaho lost most of their pony herd and sixty of their scalps to their Pawnee enemies. It was Connor's only successful engagement in Wyoming, due largely to the martial skills of his Pawnee and Omaha scouts.

In Colorado, Black Kettle's Southern Cheyenne still sought peace. Through the efforts of their friend and brother, William Bent, the Cheyenne signed a treaty with the whites they no longer trusted in October, 1865. Throughout the Dakota Territory skirmishes between the Cheyenne, Sioux and the army continued well into the next year in places called Medicine Lodge and Powder River. The army avoided major disasters only because of the Indians' inadequate fire power.

---

[105] *The Life of George Bent*, p. 227.

The U.S. Government continued its build up of supplies and troops to Wyoming's frontier. Their orders: build a string of forts along the Bozeman Trail. The "Trail," founded by cattleman John Bozeman, was the most direct route to Montana's gold fields. This new intrusion of white miners into the Sioux and Northern Cheyenne's heartland resulted in America's first massacre of soldiers from which emerged no survivors.

In 1866, the U.S. Army established Fort Phil Kearny near present day Sheridan, Wyoming. Commanded by Colonel Henry B. Carrington, its specific purpose, protect Bozeman Trail travelers from hostile attack. During the fort's short existence, work parties from the post were continually attacked and harassed by the Sioux and Cheyenne. In one such engagement, Governor Evan's old informant, Bob North, led a charge against the army with an Arapaho war party. Protecting themselves, Fort Phil Kearny's workmen fired on North, shooting a finger from his left hand. He survived northern Wyoming's war but was hanged in Kansas three years later, along with his wife, by vigilantes.

Late autumn of 1866 had frozen around Fort Phil Kearny. With the arrival of winter's solstice, Margaret Carrington, the commandant's wife, described the day's opening scene in her journal as, "Though the snow covered the mountains, and there was every indication of the return of severe weather, the morning was quite pleasant. Men wore only blouses at their work."[106] The snow from around the fort had melted, but deep drifts of winter's white harvest still lay in the woods as Big Piney Creek remained motionless in its frozen state. Around 11:00 a.m., the fort's lookout received a message: the wood cutting party was under heavy attack. Colonel Carrington ordered Captain William Fetterman to "support the wood train . . . relieve it and report to me. Do not engage or pursue Indians at its expense. Under no circumstances pursue over the ridge, that is Lodge Trail Ridge."[107]

Captain William Fetterman, a highly decorated Civil War veteran before his transfer to Fort Phil Kearny, distinguished himself in battles called Stone's River, Kennesaw Mountain and Peach Tree Creek, but he had never before fought Indians. Upon his arrival at Fort Phil Kearny, Fetterman renewed an old friendship with Captain Frederick Brown. The two men knew each other from

---

[106] *Absaraka: Home of the Crows*, p. 200.
[107] U.S. Congress 50th, 1st Session, Senate Executive Document, pp. 33, 40.

their Ohio days and the Civil War. Brown immediately oriented Fetterman with life at the fort and disclosed his personal dislike for its commanding officer. It didn't take his friend long to agree. In a letter to a friend, written in November, Fetterman described the land, weather, and the incompetence of his commanding officer, Colonel Carrington. He also wrote of his disdain for the Sioux and Cheyenne. It was obvious, at another time he bragged he could take eighty men and march through the entire Sioux nation.

The price of Fetterman's arrogance was his life. When he left Fort Phil Kearny's gates, he and the eighty men of his command went to relieve the wood train. Disregarding his specific orders from Colonel Carrington, the vain-glorious captain was lured into an ambush by Sioux decoys. Fetterman and his troops followed them beyond Lodge Trail Ridge. When they reached the ridge's top, they met a force of over one thousand Sioux, Cheyenne and Arapaho warriors. The battle lasted less than an hour and could be heard within the fort's confines. Margaret Carrington wrote, "Every shot could be heard, and there was little doubt that a desperate fight was going on in the valley of Peno Creek beyond the ridge."[108] When it was over, Fetterman and his command of eighty men were dead! No wounded or prisoners survived winter's first day of 1866. Until Custer's death nine and one-half years later, this was the United States Army's worst defeat by Indians.

All in Fetterman's command were horribly mutilated. When the relief column went out to retrieve the bodies, Colonel Carrington reported that,

> Eyes were torn out and laid on rocks; noses cut off; ears cut off; chins hewn off; teeth chopped out; joints of fingers, brains taken out and placed on rocks with other members of the body; entrails taken out and exposed; hands cut off; feet cut off; arms taken out of sockets; private parts severed and indecently placed on the person; eyes, ears, mouth, and arms penetrated with spear-heads, sticks and arrows; ribs slashed to separation with knives; skulls severed in every form, from chin to crown, muscles in calves, thighs, stomach, breast, back, arms, and cheek taken out. Punctures upon every sensitive part of the body, even the soles of the feet and the palms of the hand.[109]

---

[108] *Absaraka: Home of the Crows*, p. 203.
[109] U.S. Congress 40th, 1st Session, Senate Executive Document, pp. 33, 41.

One soldier was found, "scalped, stripped and mutilated . . . it looked as though they had stripped him first and then filled his body with arrows, as they were sticking out of him all over like porcupine quills . . . "[110] Again Margaret Carrington summed up that day in her journal as,

> All the bodies lay along or near a narrow divide over which the road ran, and to which no doubt the assailed party had retreated when overwhelming numbers bore down upon them. Captains Fetterman and Brown were at the point nearest the fort, each with a revolver shot in the left temple, and so scorched with powder as to leave no doubt that they shot each other when hope had fled. So ended the lives that were full of pride and confidence in the morning."[111]

The butchery at Sand Creek taught the Cheyenne and Sioux well, imitation was their highest form of flattery.

The war with the Northern Cheyenne and Sioux continued for two more years. However, two months prior to Fetterman's death, George Bent returned to Black Kettle's Southern Cheyenne village and married the old chief's niece, Magpie. During this period Edward (Tall Chief) Wynkoop resigned his army commission and became the Southern Cheyenne and Arapaho's Indian Agent. Through Wynkoop's work and respect for a people he loved, an uneasy peace came to this land. The tranquility of that fragile treaty was lost for a while when an eastern general, Winfield Scott Hancock, burned a Cheyenne village.

Then, on November 6, 1868, something extraordinary happened. In Wyoming's Powder River area, the United States Army, for the first time in its history, was forced to make peace with the Sioux nation. The two years since Fetterman's disaster, Red Cloud, his Oglalas and the Cheyenne out-maneuvered and out-fought the U. S. Army. President Andrew Johnson and the Congress demanded Ulysses S. Grant's best friend, William Tecumseh Sherman, the man who had led one of the most powerful armies in history on a path of destruction from Atlanta to the sea only four years earlier, make peace with an enemy his troops could not defeat.

Feeling a lasting peace was at hand, twenty-six days later, exactly four years to the day after the Sand Creek Massacre, Edward Wynkoop resigned his position as Indian Agent. He was unaware

---

[110] *The Fetterman Massacre*, Chapter 9, Murphy footnote 390.
[111] *Absaraka: Home of the Crows*, p. 208.

Magpie with husband, George Bent.

Photo courtesy Colorado Historic Society

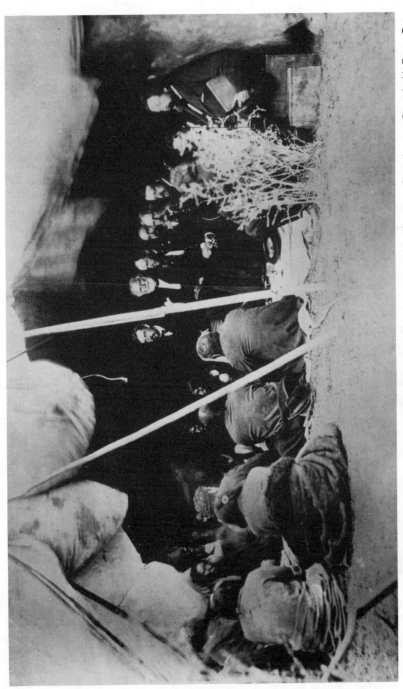

Peace Commission Ft. Laramie, 1868. L-R: Gen. S. F. Tappan, Gen. W. S. Harney, Gen. Wm. Sherman, Gen. Augua, Gen. A. H. Terry, Gen. N. G. Taylor.

Photo courtesy Wyoming State Museum

history had already repeated itself two days prior to his resignation. On November 27, 1868, Black Kettle and his people were again at peace with the United States and were camped by a river they called "Washita," in what is now western Oklahoma. This time, George Bent and his wife Magpie were not present in the village. Whether memories of what happened at Sand Creek almost four years before made him leave or whether fate had intervened and this was not his day to die is unknown. But George and his wife were safely on their way to visit his father in Colorado. There were other survivors of Sand Creek's tragedy, though, who were not as fortunate. Out of his most horrible nightmares, Black Kettle and his wife awoke to the reality — it was happening again! Between the first light and the dawn, another U.S. Cavalry troop, led by Lt. Colonel George Armstrong Custer, charged into their village and killed 101 people, most of whom were again women and children running for cover. And, as before at Sand Creek, an American flag flew over their village for protection that never came. This time, Black Kettle and his wife did not survive. When the shooting started, Moke-Tavato, Black Kettle, jumped on his horse and pulled his wife up behind him in a desperate escape attempt. It was too late though. He and Medicine Calf were shot to pieces. Their lifeless bodies fell into the Washita's cold, shallow waters. While the fight for survival continued among the living, Death's indignities were splashed on Black Kettle and Medicine Calf by the hooves of horses caught in combat. Soon after, one of Custer's soldiers appeared with a knife in his hand and cut off the great Sutai's scalp. The Cheyenne had lost a great chief and Wynkoop, a very dear friend.

Custer and his men did not stop their slaughter with human beings. He and his men shot between six hundred to nine hundred ponies, and then burned all of the Cheyenne lodges and their possessions. Custer then retreated, leaving twenty of his own troopers behind, entrapped in the remains of the village. The enraged Cheyenne cut them to pieces. Six years later, on June 25, 1876, Custer and two hundred twenty-five men of the U.S. Seventh Cavalry paid for the sins he committed on the banks of the Washita River. They all died at the hands of the Cheyenne and Sioux at another river called Little Big Horn. It was a great day for the Indians, but a bad one for Custer's family. Accompanying George on that fateful day were his two brothers, Tom and Boston. It was the worst defeat in U.S. Army history at the hands of Native American people. It was the second battle in which there were no white survivors!

12
A Tainted Wind

There's a story that I've been told
Of the greed and lust of man.
It's a story that is very old,
And it's been told since time began.

Since the beginning of time, mankind has been plagued by bigotry, racism, greed and hate. This apocalyptic quartet has sung
a song over and over again, accompanied by war's drums and
bugles, and atrocity is its common refrain.

The atrocities committed against the Cheyenne and Arapaho
did not start nor end with Sand Creek, neither did the depredations committed against the innocent whites who inadvertently
found themselves in the middle of a war. But history's unwritten
rule reflects the vanquished shall only inherit misery and despair.
And their conquerors shall rejoice in the women's lamentation, for
their mourning shall be a sweet song of tribute.

In the years between Custer's attack at the Washita River and
his death at Little Big Horn, the government sent most of the
Southern Cheyenne to various reservations established under the
guidance of the Friends of Society. U.S. Grant's administration
created the Indian Territory in what is presently the State of
Oklahoma. Their concept of a reservation and its reality was a huge
shock to the Cheyenne. The Indian Territory's hot and exception-
ally arid climate proved very alien compared to the Cheyenne's
traditional verdant prairie land. In some areas, the Cheyenne and
Arapaho found the water too brackish for their ponies' survival.
Their Quaker agents wanted to transform them into farmers and

139

teach the Cheyenne to perform all sorts of manual labor. These white Christians obviously possessed no knowledge of their new wards' customs. Farming went against hundreds of years of Cheyenne tradition. The Quakers also insisted Indian children be sent to agency schools. After months of no cooperation, the Friends finally realized verbal communication with the Cheyenne might help their problem, so they hired interpreters. But even with oral communication available, the Cheyenne warrior societies refused to become farmers. At first there were no open hostilities at the agency; their schools remained empty of Indian children. The Cheyenne remained at peace, but were adamant about their children not becoming like any of the whites they'd seen and fought for so many years.

In 1870, George Bent and his wife Magpie were among the residents at the first of these agencies, the Darlington agency (presently El Reno, Oklahoma). Agent Brinton Darlington, a Quaker for whom the agency was named, hired Bent as an interpreter. There, Little White Man's son worked to ensure no communication gap existed for the Cheyenne and Arapaho in their talks. Life for George and Magpie remained peaceful and prosperous for about two years. Then, Kiowa warriors arrived at the agency and tried to convince the Cheyenne and Arapaho to go on the warpath with them. The white man's progress created new encroachments on what little remained of their way of life. The Kiowa felt it was time to rise up and put a halt to those who sought more of their ever dwindling domain. Tempted as many of the young warriors were, the Cheyenne declined.

Not long after the Kiowas' visit tensions did mount. Numerous bands of horse thieves, who operated out of Dodge City, Kansas, preyed upon the reservation's pony herds. Completely ruthless, their outlaw raids became more commonplace and violent. Even George Bent's herd was stolen. Not wanting another war, the Cheyenne complained and asked for protection. But since the beginning of time when man first created war, the story has always been the same — the words of the vanquished have always fallen on deaf ears.

Eventually, the Southern Cheyenne and Arapaho sent a delegation to Washington, D.C., to meet with President U. S. Grant. The "Great White Father with the Whiskey Breath" listened intently to Little Robe and other delegates. He said he understood their plight and would help them, for he, the Great White Father knew and despised war above all others. He reminded them, he once commanded the largest army the world had ever seen. Grant promised Little Robe and the others protection, but his promise was like the wind in buffalo grass — nothing would come of it.

The following year, as the "Iron Horse" rode through their lands, the remainder of the last great buffalo herds were literally cut in half by this man-made beast's rails. With the railroad came more white settlers, and even more obscene to the Indians: organized bands of buffalo hunters. These hunters immediately subjected the southern herd to a slaughter the world never forgot. The quarry for which they came were the buffalo hides the great beasts possessed. After they killed their game and removed the hide, they left the carcasses to rot in the sun. The sight of this senseless slaughter sickened the plains Indians as it beckoned vultures to finish off the hide hunters' claim.

The Cheyenne and Arapaho looked on in disbelief. To them, the buffalo represented life itself. It was their belief Heammawhio created the buffalo for their use. They made their lodges, as well as winter moccasins and robes, from the hides for protection against the cold; they also molded shields as well as parfleche cases, saddle covers and cradles for the young. From the horns of this beast, the Cheyenne sculptured spoons and dishes and from the head's long hair, they made ropes and lariats. The meat provided the mainstay of their diet, and from the heavy shoulder blades, the Cheyenne carved tools for dressing the hides. The brains, liver and fat were used in tanning the hides and sinew became their thread. They wasted no part of the animal they revered. Even the tail was used to create handles for clubs and medicine wands, and the hooves produced their glue.

The Cheyenne remained at peace for a time as they witnessed the destruction of their food, clothing and tools. They hoped President Grant would keep his promise of protection. The raids on their pony herds continued though, and the buffalo's non-stop slaughter by white hunters coupled with the Cheyenne's dissatisfaction with the Indian agency's distribution of supplies finally forced them into action.

In 1874, in the Texas panhandle on Canadian River's South Fork, the hide hunters became even more bold when they established themselves in the heart of Indian hunting grounds. The site they chose was an abandoned trading fort called "Adobe Walls," which ironically was built and operated by William Bent as a sometimes trading post around 1842. The fort had been deserted for years, as Bent felt it was located too far south for his purposes.

The hide hunters' presence at this location infuriated a Comanche medicine man named Isatai (whose name translates into English as Rear-End-of-a-Wolf). Isatai claimed he possessed supernatural powers and could make the white man's bullets useless. Through his oratories and haranguing, this medicine man ignited a warring faction of the Comanches into action. The word soon spread to other tribes — the Kiowa, Arapaho and Cheyenne. Small bands from each of these tribes finally agreed to make war on these white men who, by 1872–73, had already killed in excess of two hundred thousand buffalo.

Isatai and a Comanche leader, named Quanah[112] planned to raid these hunters. The course of their action called for Comanche, Kiowa, Cheyenne and Arapaho warriors to attack them at Adobe Walls before dawn's first light. Had it not been for the heat created by the Texas night combined with the thickly insulated adobe walls, causing some of the hunters to sleep just outside in wagons, their scheme may have succeeded. When the combined Indian forces attacked, hunters in the wagons were awakened first and started firing back before the Indians could gain entry into the compound.

Inside Bent's old trading post walls, twenty-six buffalo hunters including Billy Dixon and future western lawman, gambler and sports writer, Bat Masterson, found themselves greatly outnumbered. Fortunately for the hunters, they possessed an advantage. Within their reach was an amazing arsenal of weapons and ammunition they used for their methodical slaughter of buffalo. In their well-made plans, the hunters chose the heavily fortified walls for protection against the chance for such an attack. The walls could not be shot through or burned. To make matter worse for the

---

[112]Quanah (Parker), like George Bent, was of mixed blood. His mother, Cynthia Ann Parker, was the niece of Fort Smith's famous "Hanging Judge" Isaac Parker. Two months after the Alamo's fall, Cynthia was taken by Comanches in a Texas raid, at age nine. When she was 18, Cynthia married Peta Nocona, a Comanche chief. During the next nine years she gave birth to three children — two sons, Quanah and Pecos and a daughter, Topasannah. She lived as a Comanche for twenty-four years. In 1860, she returned to the whites the same way she had been taken — in a raid. Four years after her return to the white world, Cynthia died after her daughter passed away from a fever. In her grief, Cynthia Ann Parker starved herself to death. It was said her son Quanah became a great warrior because his mother had been taken from him by whites when he was fifteen years old. He never forgave the whites for this and never saw his mother again.

Indians, the hunters barricaded the closed gates with a heavy pile of buffalo robes and their wagons. The furious fighting lasted for hours. When it was over, not a single white hunter had been killed or wounded, but eleven Indians, including five Cheyenne warriors; Horse Rode, Walks on Ground, Spotted Feathers, Coyote, and Stone Teeth, lay dead within feet of Adobe Walls' gates. Isatai's medicine had failed. As the Cheyenne and others retreated, they must have thought his name appropriate for his scheme. Before they departed however, they captured or killed most of the hunters' horses. A few days after the fighting was over, Prairie Chief and a party of Cheyenne returned to Adobe Walls. The hunters had vacated the fort's protection, but they left behind a gruesome reminder of the fight. Nine heads of the warriors killed had been severed and "stuck on boards nailed to a long pole in the ground."[113]

Their failure at Adobe Walls quickly disillusioned a majority of the Arapaho warriors who followed Isatai and returned to the agency. The Cheyenne, though, were eager to continue the fight. They preferred death in battle to death by starvation. On July 3, near present day Hennessy, Oklahoma, a Cheyenne war party attacked Patrick Hennessy (a freighter for whom the town was named) and his small wagon train. Hennessy's friend George Bent warned him not to make the trip. He tried to tell Hennessy about the multi-tribal war parties raiding the area. Hennessy, a fearless man, refused to listen and departed in spite of Bent's advice. Hennessy and his three teamsters were killed. Their bodies were discovered by Osage buffalo hunters who, in turn, threw the corpses into the teamster's wagons and burned them.

The army dispersed four columns of troops to scour the countryside in hot pursuit of the hostiles. They relentlessly followed the Cheyennes' every move for months. The troops were so close to the warring Comanches and Cheyenne, the Indians found it almost impossible to resupply during those months. Before summer ended, an additional eight troops of cavalry, four companies of infantry and artillery, under the command of Colonel Nelson A. Miles, were on the Cheyenne's trail. The hostiles discovered this white leader tenaciously dogged their every move and maneuver. The Army ordered him west following the Civil War, for Miles had already established his reputation as a fierce fighter.

---

[113] *The Life of George Bent*, p. 360.

The Cheyenne later learned that this man Miles had been the cruel jailer of Jefferson Davis, the Confederacy's ex-president. At the Civil War's climax, Union forces captured Davis while attempting to escape Richmond's fall. Under orders, the twenty-six-year-old Miles imprisoned the Confederate leader at Fort Monroe in Virginia. Miles kept Davis chained to a wall in a cold, dank cell with only a single barred window to allow the light of day to enter. For two years, Davis was subjected to petty tortures. At night, Miles ordered a light kept burning in Davis' cell, as two soldiers continuously paced beside his single cot, twenty-four hours a day. The persistency and wrath of this man now fell upon the Cheyenne.

Four years later, Miles would chase 278 half-starved Northern Cheyenne over 1,500 miles from Oklahoma to Montana. Within fifteen years, this former crockery clerk became the United States Army's Commander-in-Chief and directed the campaigns against all of the west's Indian tribes until they were killed, imprisoned, or put on reservations.

However throughout August of 1874, Miles with his Delaware scouts continued to haunt the very trails the hostile Cheyenne and Comanche followed daily. On the 31st day of that month, he caught up with them at the Washita River's headwaters and engaged them in a running fight. One Cheyenne was killed. To put some distance between themselves and the U.S. Army, the Cheyenne put their trust in a Comanche guide named Mule Smoking. This Comanche guided the Cheyenne through an area unfamiliar to them. He knew all of the water holes in this region known as the Staked Plains. Their good luck to have this guide soon turned to disaster when he became the first casualty in another running fight with Miles' troops. These skirmishes and raids continued for most of summer and early autumn, in present day Oklahoma and the Texas panhandle.

Meanwhile in mid-September, a unique Cheyenne war party roamed western Kansas' Smoky Hill River area. Its leader was Medicine Water, and with him was his wife, the woman warrior known as Mochi or Buffalo Calf Woman. In the ten years since her escape from Sand Creek's carnage Mochi lived her life as a mother and a warrior, participating in raids and pitched battles from western Kansas to Wyoming's Powder River where she counted coup and killed many of her enemies. Many stories and songs spoke of her valor in battle, how one time she rode into the midst of a Pawnee war party and rescued her brother who had had his horse shot out from under him. The Cheyenne named this battle, "The time the girl saved her brother from the Pawnee."[114] But the winds of fortune and time were running out for both Mochi and her husband. On this hot September day, her war party attacked a white family, named Germain,[115] that was traveling from Georgia to Colorado. Mochi and the other warriors killed John Germain, his wife and oldest daughter. Cheyenne war customs forbade them to take any full-grown male prisoners. They killed the two women in their initial attack, their deaths were merciful compared to the ordeal their four remaining daughters endured. When word of the killings and the girls' abduction reached the army, Colonel Miles ordered his troops to step up their patrols. Until the Germain sisters were found and their kidnappers brought to justice, Miles would not let his troops or the hostiles rest. It was the beginning of the end for the Cheyenne's last war in the south.

For two months, Medicine Water and his band avoided capture. His war party and the four white captives suffered many hardships; game was extremely scarce — the buffalo hunters had performed their jobs well. To the Indians, the appearance of Miles' pursuing troops seemed to replaced the buffalo's disappearance throughout the countryside. The Indians were kept constantly on the run. During their flight from Miles' "blue coats," Medicine Water's band sought out Gray Beard's camp on McClellan Creek in the east Texas panhandle. When they arrived, they found a village of 110 lodges. On the morning of November 8, the Cheyenne camp was discovered by Lieutenant F.D. Baldwin, and he attacked the village without warning. All of the Cheyenne who were gathered there broke camp abruptly, leaving behind two of the Germain sisters. In the midst of their departure, the Cheyenne rear guard posted themselves on a hill and waited until they saw the girls rescued by the soldiers. The two elder girls remained with the Cheyenne for two more months.

During "Hik' o min i," the Freezing Moon (November), ten years after the massacre at Sand Creek, the winter and white soldiers were rapidly approaching the Cheyenne. The harshness of 1874–75 winter caused Comanche and Kiowa warriors to return to Fort Sill and surrender. But the Cheyenne, outnumbered, cold and hungry, still refused to submit to white authority. They held out

---

[114]The Cheyenne and other plains tribes named their battles after a person's deed or death in a fight with an enemy, unlike the whites who named their battles after places.
[115]Also listed as "the German" family by some historians.

until January, 1875, when Agent John Miles sent out friendly Cheyenne runners from Darlington to find the hostiles. Their task was to induce the warriors to return to the agency. When the runners found their brothers, they were shocked at their condition. The Cheyenne's constant running from troops and their attempting to sustain themselves on little food had taken its toll. Because of the late winter cold and hunger, Agent Miles' messengers convinced most of the Cheyenne to return. Finally, White Horse and Stone Calf agreed to return with the Dog Soldiers. Accompanying Stone Calf's group were the two Germain sisters. The following month, Stone Calf and Red Moon were sent out to contact the remaining hostiles and in early March, Gray Beard and the majority of Cheyenne turned themselves in. Among the last to surrender were Medicine Water and his wife Mochi, the woman warrior. The Cheyenne war of 1874-75 was over, but the ordeal of its warriors had just begun.

Having spent two years of his military career as a jailer, Colonel Nelson A. Miles and others decided the most effective way to handle the leaders of this Indian war was to imprison them. Without a trial or tribunal, the leaders of each tribe were arrested and a decision was made to escort them to the military prison at Fort Marion, Florida.[116] Twenty-six Kiowa, nine Comanche, two Arapaho and thirty-one Cheyenne were selected. The Army's course of action completely puzzled the Indians. In their custom, any warrior or grown man taken in battle was promptly killed. It was expected and understood as a misfortune of war. But to be placed in chains and put into a prison was unacceptable to their beliefs. To the Cheyenne, suicide was not an option either since they had been taught their "tassoom" or spirit would be doomed to walk the earth forever.

Some say Lieutenant Colonel Thomas H. Neill was drunk the day he selected the Cheyenne to be imprisoned.[117] The hard drinking career officer first chose the leaders, Gray Beard, Heap of Birds (Many Magpies), Eagle Head, Lean Bear (the son of the old chief killed in 1863), Medicine Water and Mochi, the woman warrior. Neill chose her because Sophia Germain, the youngest surviving girl, accused Mochi as the person who, "chopped my mother's head

---

[116]Fifty years ago the United States Park Service changed the name of Fort Marion to The Castillo de San Marcos and Fort Mantanzas National Monuments, located in St. Augustine, Florida.
[117]*The Life of George Bent*, p. 365.

open with an ax."[118] From there, Neill decided to "cut off eighteen from the right of the line;" only the number of Cheyenne, including the chiefs involved, to be sent to prison was important. Many of the "eighteen" were innocent of any wrong doing, but to Colonel Neill, the point was moot.

The morning of April 6, 1875 was not a routine day for Darlington's blacksmith. The Army ordered Wesley, a large, powerful, former slave, to place the thirty-one prisoners in leg irons. As he started his unpleasant task, he may have remembered his own days of being chained. Whether the memories of those days or the sound of Cheyenne women singing nearby caused him to become uncomfortable, it is unknown. Neither he nor the others present were aware the women's song actually taunted the warriors being chained. Their song scorned the warriors with, "Where will we get fathers worth giving sons to? We see there are no men among you worth taking to our beds!"[119] After having placed several of the Cheyenne into irons, the former slave now confronted a warrior whose battle exploits were near legendary. He stood about 5 feet-11 inches and weighed about 185 pounds. Although the muscled warrior was smaller than Wesley, he possessed a massive barrel chest and looks that belied his quickness and agility. His name was Black Horse (named in honor of old chief Black Horse, the man who helped defeat Fetterman's troops near Fort Phil Kearny nine years earlier). As Wesley attempted to place him in irons, Black Horse kicked him under the chin and ran for his life. Through a hail of the guard's gunfire, Black Horse bolted to open ground beyond the agency's confines. Running as though he were a brother to the prairie wind itself, Black Horse seemed impervious to the bullets flying around him. He felt he could reach the safety of White Horse's camp in the distance. When he was about thirty yards from the camp, Black Horse was knocked to the ground. One of the soldier's bullets had found its mark in Black Horse's side.

He was not alone in his break from the army. Others not yet ironed broke and fled for their freedom. Some of them ran to the fallen Black Horse's aid and dragged him to safety.[120] Well aimed

---

[118]*The Southern Cheyenne*, p. 401.
[119]*Cheyenne Autumn*, p. 115.
[120]Army reports state that Black Horse was "killed." But George Bent, who was present, stated Black Horse was only wounded. Other Cheyenne present that day told of Black Horse's survival, including interviews done by Mari Sandoz for her book *Cheyenne Autumn*. The Book *Cheyenne Memories*, a Cheyenne oral history, also indicates Black Horse survived and fought on for the next couple of years.

"indiscriminate" bullets fired through the camp again found innocent victims. Several women and children were wounded by guards trying to cut down the fleeing Cheyenne prisoners. In a panic, more women and children scurried for the sand hills beyond the Cheyenne camp and began to dig pits in which to escape the slaughter. White Horse's men were poorly armed, but they gathered what rifles and bows and arrows they possessed and dug in for the troops' impending attack. The army, now in force, brought up a Gatling gun for extra fire power.

The younger Cheyenne men moved beyond their camp as the fighting commenced in earnest and dug up the guns they had hidden before the army disarmed them. As the Cheyenne scooped out dirt with their hands to make their position stronger, the wounded Black Horse dragged himself along to the people shouting, "Hold fast!" and "Fight Hard!" Then he sang:

> The women will see they still have men
> To father their sons
> We will not sit in chains!
> It is better to die fighting.[121]

The troops then charged the sand hills position, but they were turned back due to the entrenched Cheyennes' accurate shooting. As the Indians' resistance intensified the army wheeled forward a Gatling gun and opened fire onto the sand hills. The weapon's barrels spewed its unearthly deluge of bullets into the Cheyenne position. Fortunately, the rounds could not penetrate the sand, but its shocking effects terrified many the women and children who took refuge there. Black Horse and other warriors prevented complete pandemonium. Nightfall found the Cheyenne completely surrounded by the army. However, as the troops awaited daylight to finish their job, the Cheyenne, under darkness' cover, slipped silently through the surrounding troops and vanished into the night. The following day, the troops were astonished that all of the Cheyenne men, women and children had escaped their tightly woven net around the sand hills.

The Cheyenne refugees soon forged their way north to escape the starvation and chains the Indian Territory held for them. Within three days of their Darlington escape, they encountered a group of hostiles who had not yet surrendered. Their leader, Little

---

[121] *Cheyenne Autumn*, p. 116.

Bull had been out all winter. He and his group were on their way to Darlington to surrender. Confronted with the tales of slaughter occurring at the agency, Little Bull and the fleeing Cheyenne held a brief council. About twenty lodges decided to make a run for it with the others, while another faction in camp persuaded some of Little Bull's party to return to the agency.

Little Bull, Chicken Hawk, Spotted Wolf and White Horse decided their safety lay in the north country. They would rather fight to the death than be ironed and caged in a land the whites called Florida. During this time, the army had notified its forts in Kansas to be on the lookout for the fleeing Cheyenne. At Fort Wallace, Kansas, Lieutenant Austin Henely's orders were to head off the Indians and prevent their escape into Nebraska.

After crossing the Smoky Hill River, the Cheyenne again found the army on their trail. Thus, they split into small parties to confuse the pursuing troops. Though they managed to puzzle the troopers time and again, the Cheyenne could not lose them. Little Bull's party decided to camp on the North Fork of Sappa Creek, in the northwest part of Kansas. This creek was a good place to hide because of its isolated location, and had it not been for blind luck, Lieutenant Henely would never have found them. On April 22, 1875, Lieutenant Henely met a group of white buffalo hunters who had seen the Indian camp on Sappa Creek. With thoughts of plundering the village, the hunters agreed to guide Henely and his troops to the creek.

At daybreak on April 23rd, Henely's troops attacked the Cheyenne. As the fighting commenced, his troops rushed across the creek and took positions where they unleashed a murderous cross fire into the village. The buffalo hunters fired their powerful, long-range rifles so rapidly the Cheyenne looked as if they were being executed. Many of their targets were women and children. Little Bull had seen enough. He and Dirty Water finally ventured out to parley with Henely. The lieutenant sent out a sergeant to meet with the two Cheyenne. As the sergeant approached the two men, a warrior named White Bear rose up from his position of cover and fired his rifle. The sergeant died before he knew he'd been shot. Without hesitation or an order, the troops opened fire, killing Little Bull and Dirty Water instantly. The sounds of battle again filled the Kansas countryside. The army's fire power and the buffalo hunters' accuracy was so intense the Cheyenne were forced to withdraw. Many escaped through this lead torrent to forge their way north but White Bear was not one of them. As he rose up to take a final shot at the army and exposed himself to the murderous fire, he was killed. Little Bear also died at Sappa Creek. His mother and father were killed earlier in the fight. In his final act of defiance he jumped upon his pony and charged into the troop's position. The army riddled his body with bullets; only his pony survived the fight. Twenty-seven Cheyenne died that day.

The official U.S. Army reports stated nineteen warriors and eight women and children died on April 23, 1875. The Cheyenne said the only men killed that day were Little Bull, Dirty Water, Tangle Hair, The Rat, White Bear, Young Bear, and Stone Teeth. The other twenty persons killed were women and children.

Black Horse survived the fight at Sappa Creek. He and the other Cheyenne escaped to the north country. Starvation and exposure to the elements punctuated the ordeal they suffered in their 1,500 mile journey in the time they called "The Fat Moon." Black Horse survived to fight another day. He counted coup and killed many of his enemies on a June day one year later, the time when the Cheyenne and Sioux met "Yellow Hair" Custer on the banks of the Little Big Horn River in Montana. They remembered him from the Washita River, eight years before.

Black Horse's exploits survived the man who died in 1936. In his lifetime he fought against the soldiers wherever he found them and raided ranches and farms for years. He eventually settled down at the Northern Cheyenne Reservation in Lame Deer, Montana. He was married three times during his lifetime.[122]

---

[122]Almost twenty years after his death, his great-grandson, Ben Nighthorse Campbell, became a decorated Korean War veteran. In the early 1960's, Campbell became a three times U.S. Open Champion in Judo and was a captain of the U.S. Judo team in the 1964 Olympics. Campbell is also a highly recognized artist in silver and turquoise. He served for years in the State Legislature of Colorado and today, Ben Nighthorse Campbell is only the seventh Native American ever to serve in the United States Congress and is presently the only one serving. It is not surprising that he is free of the many controversies that have been woven through the corridors of Capitol Hill in Washington, D.C. For in the tradition of his people, honor is important, and that is why they made him a chief of the Northern Cheyenne.

In 1991, Congressman Campbell proposed a bill to the U.S. Congress that would officially change the name of the Custer Battlefield to the Little Bighorn Battlefield. It passed the House of Representatives and the Senate that same year. In December, the name change became official, a tribute to the men of both races who fought and died there so long ago.

13
And Those Who Survived...

There is a song
In Life we sing:
That history will judge you
For what you bring.

The Twilight Years of the Cheyenne

For the thirty-one Cheyenne prisoners who were ironed and
sentenced to Fort Marion, Florida, life changed from their reality
to a fantasy world. The Bureau of Indian Affairs ordered Captain
Richard Henry Pratt, a young Civil War veteran, to escort the
prisoners by train to their Florida destination. Pratt personally felt
Indians were people and not savages. This feeling was unique
among officers in the United States Army. His intentions for the
Cheyenne and other Indian prisoners in his custody were positive,
but some what misguided in the direction he took. Pratt felt if he
could take the "Indian out of the man," the man could be salvaged
and made into a brown-skinned replica of a White, Anglo-Saxon
Protestant. Before implementing his idea, however, his first task was
to get his "wards" to prison.

The Indians never forgot their train ride to Florida. For most, it
was their first close encounter with the "Iron Horse." The Cheyenne
and other prisoners, still in their irons were put in rail cars. The

151

thousand mile trip to where the sun "rises from the earth" seemed endless. Pratt tried to make his presence known to the prisoners a few times a day, not in the role of overlord, but rather as a benevolent caretaker. During one of his tours, Captain Pratt, accompanied by his six-year-old daughter, came in contact with Gray Beard. The Cheyenne chief, speaking through an interpreter, asked the captain in a trembling voice, "How would you like to have chains on your legs, as I have and be taken a long distance from your home, your wife and little girl, as I have?"[123] Pratt was silent; this was not a question he could easily answer. Gray Beard found his absolution however, not with the spoken word, but through the smell of gunpowder.

As the train neared the Georgia-Florida state line, one of the guards awoke Pratt and told him a prisoner had escaped. Pratt pulled the emergency cord to stop the train, and as it jarred to a halt, he told the conductor what had happened. During the search, Pratt discovered Gray Beard had freed himself from his chains and jumped from the train through his open window. The Cheyenne had taken his blanket and bundle and seemingly had vanished into the humid southern night. Pratt ordered the train backed up, and armed troops soon scoured the Georgia countryside. Then one of the troopers, a sergeant, spotted Gray Beard's hiding place. He had jumped from the train onto a palmetto tree. As Gray Beard leaped from the tree to escape, the sergeant shouted for him to halt, but the Cheyenne spoke no English, and probably would not have stopped anyway. The sergeant took aim and shot the Cheyenne through the back. The bullet came out through his chest. Pratt noted,

> He was still living. We fixed a place and lifted him into the rear
> of the last car and brought Manimic (sic), his old friend and
> war chief and others of his tribe to see him. The interpreter
> stood by and told me what they said. Among other things Gray
> Beard said he had wanted to die ever since being chained and
> taken from home. He told Manimic what to tell his wife and
> daughter and soon died."[124]

Gray Beard was not the last to die. Upon reaching the old Spanish fort, the Cheyenne knew death was near, for outside their wall was the Atlantic Ocean. They had never seen the coast before and thought it to be the first of the four great rivers they had to cross on their way to Seyan. And when Pratt ordered the

---

[123] *Battlefield and Classroom*, Richard Henry Pratt, p. 113.
[124] Ibid., pp. 114–115.

Fort Marion prisoners. Back row, L-R: Mochi (Buffalo Calf Woman) (Cheyenne), her husband, Medicine Water (Cheyenne). Front row, L-R: Black Horse's wife (not a prisoner), Black Horse (Comanche), and Minimic (Cheyenne). Photo courtesy Luis Arana, United States Dept. of Interior

Cheyenne's hair cut as a part of their becoming "civilized," they knew great sorrow followed. Unbeknownst to Pratt, hair cutting represented great mourning for the Cheyenne. Indian blankets and beaded moccasins were traded in for army uniforms. Pratt sought to remove every aspect of their Indian life, including religion, tribal customs, language and inadvertently, their natural dignity, and transform them into the white man's image.

During their three year prison term, the Cheyenne and others were brought into St. Augustine wearing their uniforms to show the local citizens the progress they were making towards being turned into white men. The locals purchased the souvenir bows and arrows they made as well as their bead work. What little money they earned was sent back to the Darlington Agency to help their families. More often than not, their money never reached beyond the pockets of the guards they entrusted it to.

During non-working and school times, the Indians were allowed to go fishing in the Atlantic Ocean just outside the walls of their prison. They found great excitement in hunting and killing the great "Water Buffalo,"[125] which swam through the warm coastal waters. When they committed infractions they were chained and put in a dark, solitary cell for days or weeks. In one case, Pratt's medical officer sedated an uncooperative Cheyenne prisoner in front of other Indians. They thought the man to be dead. When the drug eventually wore off and the Cheyenne woke up, it convinced the Indians Pratt's "medicine" was so great, he could actually resurrect the dead. After this incident he had little trouble with the majority of his inmates.

However, following the first year of their imprisonment, the Northern Cheyenne and Sioux defeated Custer at Little Big Horn, Montana, three thousand miles away. After that shocking news reached St. Augustine's citizens, the Cheyenne and others confined at the old Spanish fort were no longer allowed their excursions into town.

When Pratt departed Fort Marion in 1879, he took his ideas of transforming Indians into whites with him. Later in 1879, his creation of the "Indian Industrial Schools," grew from the shell of an old army barracks in Carlisle, Pennsylvania. His first school was aptly named the Carlisle School for the Indians.[126] Pratt's belief that

---

[125]The Cheyenne and others referred to the many sharks they caught as "Water Buffalo."
[126]Carlisle's most famous student was Jim Thorpe. He is still considered the greatest athlete of all time. Thorpe came from the Sac-Fox nations in Oklahoma to Carlisle around 1905.

the Indians should be educated into the white man's culture was correct, however, his attempt to destroy their culture in the process was misguided. For many of the Cheyenne who returned to the reservation in Oklahoma after their imprisonment, life was a mixture of their old ways and their new religion and education. Assimilation was very difficult. Few would prosper or rise above the poverty still pervading its confines. And over the years, alcoholism induced by reservation life has killed more Cheyenne than all of the bullets in all of their wars. One reason for this deplorable statistic is the Cheyenne, along with other reservation Indians, lost their identity and their dignity while white men sought to make them a brown reflection. Those who did not leave the fort were considered lucky. During their three year imprisonment, many of the Cheyenne, Kiowa, Arapaho and Comanche died from the white man's diseases lurking in the depths and darkness of that three hundred-year-old fort.

For those who remembered, Sweet Medicine's prophecies all came true.

John Chivington

After the hearings on Sand Creek, John Chivington remained in Denver for a few years. Many in Colorado still believed him to be a hero, but many in the East thought him to be a murderer. Chivington's life never returned to normal after the hearings — and after the accidental drowning in 1866 of his son Thomas in the Platte River. In August, 1867 tragedy again struck when his wife Martha died following a long illness.

Not long after her death, a strange, one paragraph newspaper article entitled, "A WICKED WEDDING," appeared in the *Rocky Mountain News*. It simply read:

> It seems to be true that John M. Chivington has married his son's widow. What will he do next to outrage the moral sense and feeling of his day and generation, remains to be seen; but be sure it will be something, if there is anything left for him to do.

The article was one of the very few to ever criticize Chivington. It was rumored the marriage, undertaken without the consent of the girl's parents, lasted only two weeks. She fled his household because of his extreme cruelty and went back home.

Later in 1868, Chivington moved from Denver to San Diego, California. In the five years he resided there, his whereabouts were totally unknown to his Denver friends. In 1873, he returned to Warren County, Ohio. There he married Mrs. Isabella Arnsen, a wealthy Cincinnati widow. After his newly acquired farm burned, John purchased a home and the Blanchester Press in neighboring Clinton County. Chivington again tried his hand at politics and ran for the Ohio state legislature as a Republican. He withdrew from the race, probably because of pressure from the predominate group in the area, the Quakers. Their sympathetic views towards the Indians made them disapprove of Chivington's actions at Sand Creek.

Chivington returned to Denver ten years later and became prominent in Colorado political circles. Still very popular, he was appointed Under Sheriff of Denver and was later elected County Coroner. He unsuccessfully ran for the Congress of the United States in two elections. In 1894, at the age of seventy-three, after a lengthy illness, death at last claimed the life of John M. Chivington.

Controversy about this man still lives, though. Every year on the anniversary of the 29th day of November, 1864, people write to the Denver newspapers proclaiming his heroics or condemning his deeds. In a speech he delivered shortly before his death, the old colonel unrepentantly stated, "I still stand by Sand Creek." Chivington was buried in Denver, at the Fairmont Cemetery.

His legacy of hate and bigotry still lives on in many parts of Colorado. There are many who feel no massacre occurred at Sand Creek. It was, instead, a battle.

John Evans

Governor John Evans' political career ended with his part in the Sand Creek Massacre. President Andrew Johnson removed him from office in August, 1865. Washington very clearly heard the public outcry of the eastern citizenry.

Evans became a prominent businessman and educator in Colorado. In the late 1860's, Evans began funding railroads once again. When he learned the transcontinental railroad would go north through Cheyenne, Wyoming, instead of Denver, Evans assumed responsibility for building a new rail line. His line ran from Denver to Cheyenne to keep the "Mile High City" from being isolated from the railroad, thus the world.

His philanthropy helped establish Denver's educational systems and he eventually founded what is now the University of Denver.

When Evans died on July 3, 1897, the people of Colorado honored his memory with a state funeral. Streets were named after him, as well as one of the highest mountains in North America. He is still considered by many people to be one of the greatest men in Colorado history.

It is sad all of his many remarkable business, building and educational exploits will forever be tainted by the pungent wind of controversy that still blows over Sand Creek.

George Shoup

Like Chivington, Colonel George Shoup was never brought to trial for his part in the Sand Creek Massacre. Shoup commanded the Third Colorado Volunteers, the regiment responsible for most of the atrocities committed on the bloody 29th day of November.

At the end of the Civil War, Shoup left Colorado, went to Virginia City, Montana, and opened a mercantile business. Within a year of the opening his store, Shoup moved on to Idaho where he helped found the town of Salmon. There, he married and raised a family.

In 1889, Shoup became the first territorial governor, and later the first elected governor, of the new State of Idaho. Two years later, Shoup became the first U.S. Senator elected from Idaho and served at this post for ten years.

George Laird Shoup died on the first day of winter, 1904, at the age of sixty-eight.

Charlie Bent

This youngest son of William Bent renounced his white heritage and at the age of fifteen became one of the most wanted men in the west. Not only did he declare his hatred for the whites, but he also vowed to kill his father after William disowned him for the atrocities Charlie was committing throughout Colorado, Kansas and Nebraska. Luckily, the elder Bent was in New Mexico when Charlie tried to fulfill his oath. In 1868, Pawnee Indians wounded Charlie Bent in a fight. Though badly injured, he returned to his Cheyenne camp and while being treated for his wounds, he contracted malaria and died.

Edward "Tall Chief" Wynkoop

Wynkoop eventually moved to New Mexico and became the warden for the territorial prison. On September 11, 1891 he died of Bright's disease. Wynkoop was fifty-five years old.

His family moved back to Denver and when his wife, Louise, had difficulty obtaining her widow's pension, another bizarre twist of fate occurred. Wynkoop's old nemesis, John Chivington, assisted her in expediting her claim by writing a letter to the U.S. Pension Agency.

William Gilpin

William Gilpin stayed active in Colorado for the rest of his days as a businessman, a politician, a writer and an educator. On February 16, 1874, he married Julia Pratte Dickerson, the daughter of an old friend and the widow of army captain John Dickerson. Their tempestuous marriage lasted for thirteen years, and they had four children. In March of 1887, William filed for divorce. In 1891, after four years of fighting with each other in the courts, William and Julia reunited.

During his last years of life, Gilpin visited the State house almost every day. The former governor watched his dust-covered home of Denver grow out of the wilderness to become the beautiful "Queen City" of the west. He also witnessed the metamorphosis of Cheyenne and Arapaho land growing into the State of Colorado during his lifetime. On January 19, 1894, at the age of seventy-nine, William Gilpin died peacefully in his sleep. He was buried in the Mount Olivet Cemetery in Denver, very near the mountains he so dearly loved.

James P. Beckwourth

After the congressional hearings on the Sand Creek Massacre ended, Jim Beckwourth left Denver and headed for the country of his adopted tribe, the Crow. Beckwourth had been made a leader in the warrior society many years before. In 1866, Beckwourth stayed and worked at Fort Laramie for a while and later in the same year, he traveled farther north to Fort Phil Kearny, near present day Sheridan, Wyoming. During his employment with Colonel Henry Carrington, Beckwourth guided a Lieutenant Templeton into the very heart of Crow country. Templeton asked Beckwourth to go into the village they found. Before ever leaving the troop column, Beckwourth complained about headaches and suffered nosebleeds. On October 29, 1866, while in the Crow camp, he suddenly died. He was buried by the people with whom he lived and loved for over forty years.

When learning of Beckwourth's death, William Byers, the founder and publisher of the Rocky Mountain News, wrote a whopper of a tale. Never one to tell the whole truth when a great tale could be perpetuated, particularly when the story involved Indians, Byers wrote Beckwourth had been poisoned by the Crow Indians while eating dog meat with them. The reason Byers gave for the Crows performing their dastardly deed was that they feared Beckwourth's medicine and if he left them again, tragedy would befall them.

Unfortunately, this myth is still being told as gospel in many parts of Colorado. The diaries of Lieutenant Templeton, however, disprove this story, as does the fact the Crow and other western Indians did not utilize poisons to kill their enemies. Counting coup and fighting in battle were the bravest things a warrior could do. Beckwourth's death was probably due to complications brought on by hypertension.[127]

George Bent

George Bent, after renouncing his white heritage, lived with the Cheyenne for almost fifty-three years until his death in 1918. During his remarkable life amongst the Cheyenne, he was a warrior, an interpreter and a trader. George inherited his father's business mind and from the time he entered the Darlington Agency in 1870, he began investing in real estate and railroad bonds. From 1905 to 1915, he worked with anthropologist, George Bird Grinnell, interviewing elderly Cheyenne people for Grinnell's studies. And, from 1907 to shortly before his death in 1918, Bent corresponded with historian, George Hyde.

George Bent was married three times. His last wife was Standing Out Smith Bent. She gave birth to two children, a girl, Lucy, and a boy named William Henry. George's two children lived well into

---

[127]The author asked several doctors what may have caused Beckwourth's symptoms. They all said hypertension in combination with heart failure.

adulthood. Eventually, William married. His wife, Ellen Adams, gave birth to William Junior and Lucille.

The extent of George Bent's business dealings was not known until 1988 when his daughter, Lucy, died at age ninety-two in Clinton, Oklahoma. Relatives cared for Lucy for over thirty years in the shack in which she lived. As one of her granddaughters was cleaning out the shack, she found railroad stocks and deeds to properties. The estate's total value was in excess of nine million dollars. Before Lucy died she told her only niece she would inherit her belongings. But when the size of the estate was discovered, other living relatives initiated a huge lawsuit. They felt they should also have the money. One of Lucy's great-nieces tried to have her mother committed to a mental health hospital to gain control of the fortune. The suit was dismissed and the person who rightfully inherited the estate has since used the money to benefit an Indian church, an Indian senior citizens' center and the Indian hospital in the Clinton, Oklahoma area.

George Bent died at the age of seventy-five and is buried in Colony, Oklahoma. He lies forgotten to history, but his first-hand accounts of this fascinating period in the lives of the Cheyenne will live forever in libraries and archives throughout the West. Much of the information on Cheyenne customs and warfare contained in this book came directly from Bent's written pioneer accounts and from interviews with his granddaughter, Lucille Bent, and his great-granddaughter, Ann Strange Owl.

Kit Carson

Carson spent years as a scout for the army as well as a commissioned officer. After settling down with his wife, Josefa, he worked as an Indian Agent for the Ute Indians in northern New Mexico.

In May of 1868, Kit Carson visited William Bent's ranch, but Bent was in Missouri at the time. Carson was dying, some say of a broken heart, because his beloved Josefa passed away only three months earlier, giving birth to his seventh child. George Bent came to visit Carson and these two great men of the west reminisced about the early days in this land, for both men had seen the changes since those days when the white man's movement west started flooding the lands.

When William returned to his ranch, he was saddened to learn one of his oldest and dearest friends had died on the 23rd day of May.

Wilson Tamaker, great grandson of Comanche war chief Quanah Parker and Lucille Bent, granddaughter of George Bent, in the 1960s.

Photo courtesy Lucille Bent

Lucille Bent, George Bent's daughter.

Photo courtesy Lucille Bent

William "Little White Man" Bent

William Bent never strayed too far from the rich bottom lands of the Arkansas River. Although he stayed busy with his many businesses, he never got over the loss of his family. Only Robert, George and Mary stayed in touch with their father after Sand Creek's tragedy.

In 1867, William married the daughter of a Blackfoot woman and a white fur trader. Her name was Adalina Harvey. This marriage lasted only a few months and William once again resigned himself to living alone.

Almost one year to the day of Carson's death, William "Little White Man" Bent became seriously ill and was taken to his ranch near the mouth of the Purgatory River. His daughter, Mary, looked after him and sent for the doctor at Ft. Lyons.

His fever and delirium may have taken William back to those times when his adopted people, the Cheyenne, roamed free. Of this we shall never know, for Little White Man died on May 19, 1869, without ever speaking again. His family buried him in the land he loved, within miles of the "River of Lost Souls." The Cheyenne who knew and loved him are sure the Wise One Above came down and guided him across the four great rivers, then along

William Bent's home in St. Louis.   Photo courtesy Colorado Historic Society

the Milky Way's route, to the place they call Seyan, where he would once and forevermore be joined by his beloved Owl Woman.

A few days after his funeral, William's obituary appeared in the *Pueblo Chieftain.* The white man's paper told of Bent's estate and the size of his fortune but never mentioned his accomplishments as a man of the west.

In the old cemetery in Las Animas, Colorado, where he is buried, William Bent's name is carved upon a large marble monument. But Little White Man's Cheyenne legacy still lives, for long ago his name was written in the hearts of the people he loved, the Tsis Tsis Tas.

The Germain Sisters

The surviving Germain sisters were formally adopted by General Nelson A. Miles shortly after their ordeal with the Cheyenne. All eventually married and raised families. In 1990, one of Sophia Germain's great-great-granddaughters, Arlene Jauken contacted the Oklahoma Historic Society for information on the massacre of her ancestors. Ironically, the letter was forwarded to historian John L. Sipes.

At first Sipes didn't quite know how to handle the predicament he found himself in, so he finally called Mrs. Jauken in Humboldt, Nebraska, and informed her who he was and how he received her letter. Mrs. Jauken recalled,

> I was so shocked. He called me early in the morning and said, 'I'm the descendant of Medicine Water and Buffalo Calf Woman (Mochi) who killed your great-great-grandparents.' I didn't need my first cup of coffee to wake me up.[128]

On September 8, 1990, Sipes and Jauken held a reunion in the grasslands of Cheyenne County, Kansas. Cheyenne families from Colorado, Oklahoma and Montana all gathered there to pray. Later Jauken and the others participated in a peace ceremony.

"It was a tragedy for both the Germain family and the Sand Creek victims. My message will be about love and forgiveness,' Jauken said."

---

[128]News article, Knight Ridder Newspapers, Gazette Telegraph, Colorado Springs, Colorado. September 8, 1990.

Mochi and Medicine Water

While Mochi and Medicine Water were imprisoned for three years at Fort Marion, their children were left behind at the Darlington agency but were later sent to the Colony School.

During his imprisonment, the army considered Medicine Water very dangerous. At one point, he was placed in irons and chained to a dark, solitary jail cell. His guards permitted no light to enter his cell and they restricted his diet to only bread and water for a three week period.

At this writing little is known about Mochi's prison life except she was Fort Marion's only female prisoner, although some of the prisoners' wives followed them to their life of confinement and remained within the fort's walls.

In 1878, all of the surviving prisoners were released and returned to the various reservations in Oklahoma. Mochi and Medicine Water returned home to Clinton and were reunited with their family. Her years of fighting on the plains had taken its toll on her youth, both physically and mentally, while her prison life, amidst the dankness and humidity, accelerated the deterioration of her lungs and health.

In 1881, Mochi — Buffalo Calf Woman, the Cheyenne woman warrior died peacefully surrounded by her family. She was buried on a high mound, where there were no trees to build a scaffold for her journey across the four great rivers, so she might find her way to Seyan. She was only forty-one-years old. Forty five years later, Medicine Water followed Mochi to the grave. He was buried next to her in 1926. Their graves are unmarked, but are cared for by decendants who know their location. Medicine Water and Mochi were the last of the holdouts in the 1875 Cheyenne War.

14
A Return to
Sand Creek

Rising from the mists of morn
As the dawn's light makes its stand.
The wind still sings of sorrow born,
On the banks of the Big Sand.

The prairie lands of southeastern Colorado haven't changed much in the last one hundred and twenty-eight years since Yellow Wolf's death. Occasional groves of cottonwood trees dot the vast grasslands, stirring nature's memory of what she once held in abundance. Since that tragic November day in 1864, the ground on this prairie has been disturbed in many ways. Before the plows of progress turned over the land to farming and ranching, scavengers searched the ground. The dead from Sand Creek remained unburied for weeks after their brutal end. After the coyotes and vultures had finished their carnal gratification, the two legged scavengers made their first appearance. In 1867 Army surgeons arrived to collect body parts of Sand Creek's dead. Their mission was to study the effects of gunshot wounds to the body, much like the studies they had conducted on the Civil War dead. In this case the most often collected body part was the head. They simply cut the heads off the dead Cheyenne and Arapaho and threw them into a wagon. They were then shipped back to the Army Medical Museum in Washington, D.C. Funeral ornaments were also collected from the dead they found. Between 1897 and 1907, these remains and objects were transferred to the Smithsonian Institute. Recently the Smithsonian contacted leaders of the Arapaho nation, in Wyoming, to make arrangements for the return of their ancestors' remains. These collections were made throughout the Indians wars and approximately 4,000 heads and other body parts still remain at the Smithsonian Institute. But other body parts remain in private collections.

In the 1980's one former Colorado legislator often showed off a "tobacco pouch" made from the private parts of a male victim of Sand Creek to his colleagues on a regular basis. It had been in his family for generations and he used it for a candy bag. Lack of effort or conscience changed his insensitivity, but death did. This legislator passed away, but the pouch remains with his family. There are others however, who had more understanding and did not agree with their ancestor's beliefs or actions.

On a July day, 1991, five cars filled with eight people of three races were making their way down the two lane highway that now bisect this ancient land of the Tsis Tsis Tas. They had come on a sacred mission. In their possession were two Indian scalps. Connie Buffalo, a successful marketer for a laser disc company was one of the women in the caravan.

In the days prior to her pilgrimage, this very articulate and attractive Ojibwa Indian had traveled through a small Colorado town on her annual vacation to replenish her spirit. Fatigued and hungry, Connie decided to stay in the small mountain community through which she was passing, since the next town was forty miles away. Eager for rest, she pulled into a small motel. As Connie entered the establishment's lobby, she felt extremely uncomfortable. She didn't feel as though she was in danger, but Connie sensed a terrible wrong in this office. She noticed the walls were covered with early western paraphernalia. The center above the fireplace displayed an old Cheyenne arrow quiver. Connie mentioned her uneasiness to the desk clerk. The clerk replied, "maybe it's that old quiver." But Connie said she felt it was something more. The clerk then added, "maybe it's the scalps." The desk clerk then showed Connie two Indian scalps that had been sewn together, hanging behind the quiver. One of the scalps appeared to be a man's and the other seemed that of a child's. The initial shock of this sight overpowered Connie when she realized what the two objects were. One seldom sees a human scalp. These are more often the subject of stories long past. Now, with the weight of braided hair resting in her hands, the stories took on a new reality. The sadness of what man did to man in the name of war was overwhelming.

The clerk, the manager's wife, took them back with dulled automatic movements. As Connie checked in, she tried to take in the emotions of this experience. Once in her room, Connie attempted to relax, but rest eluded her. Something drew her away from her room to her car. She soon found herself driving into the vastness of the mountain-silhouetted night with no thought or direction in mind. As though guided by a spirit of the past, Connie ended her journey near a mountain lake. Surrounded by the omnipotence of summer's sky and the sounds of the lake's gentle lapping shoreline, Connie heard the voices of this ancient land cry out to her Native American mind and heart. Above and below merged into one space in time, just like the past and present merged into one feeling.

Close to the earth, in the night's silence, Connie took out her pipe to pray. She asked her ancestors to be present and she prayed to the Great Spirit for guidance. Her answer was quick as a voice within her said,

> You are to take the scalps back to Sand Creek and bury them. This must be done in a specific way. All who participate in this ceremony must come with peace in their hearts, and must pray for those who died as well as those who killed. Balance can only be restored in this way. All come from the Great Spirit and all must be held in forgiveness. You must remember that good and evil are deep within each heart. No man is separate from his brother. Then pray that all hearts come to good.

It was not time yet to work the pipe, only to weep, hear and learn.

Hours later she returned to the motel and a sleepless night. In the morning as she checked out, she inquired about the scalps. The clerk said the scalps belonged to her husband Tom, who was in the next room. In her gentle way of doing things, Connie asked if she might speak to him. The woman said, "sure, but if you want to buy them, you're out of luck. My husband won't sell. He was once offered an entire RV for them and he wouldn't trade." The motel clerk called Tom and he soon appeared. He was an older, outgoing, big man whose smile still retained the impish grin that had captivated many a young girl's heart when he was a champion cowboy. His life had been filled with whiskey, women, horses and hard work, but Tom always had a heart as big as the Rocky Mountains. After Tom got married, he almost settled down, and as he got older, he did mellow out a bit. But you'd never convince those who watched Tom and his dog Mitch. They were well known traveling companions in town. Sometimes Tom could be seen backing his old flatbed truck down the highway, looking for Mitch because the dog had either fallen or jumped off the truck. But whether Tom had his dog with him or not, many a man down on his luck always knew Tom would help in any way he could. Tom was friendly as Connie introduced herself, but his disposition changed when Connie, pointing to the scalps, said, "When you are ready, the scalps must be taken home to be buried." Tom remained silent as his wife laughed and again told Connie, when it came to those scalps, she was out of luck. Tom then told Connie his great-grandfather had been a member of Chivington's army and his ancestor had taken those scalps at Sand Creek. She listened until he finished his story and again said, "I will take the scalps home when you are ready." Silence followed, and when that silence seemed intolerable, Tom told Connie, "If I could pick a time and place to live my life over, I would choose the life of a warrior on the plains before there were white men there." Connie then quietly and gently spoke to his mountain man's heart when she asked, "Don't you think it's time for them to go home?" Tom's eyes welled with tears as he raised his will above that of his family's history. Slowly he turned away from Connie and removed the scalps from the wall. As he handed them to her he said, "I have never agreed with what happened at Sand Creek; it's just that those scalps have been in my family since that terrible time. If it means that much to you, you can have them." His voice trailed off as he fought back his tears.[129] Connie understood. Connie checked out of the motel with the scalps in her possession and crossed the street to a small general store. There she purchased some red cloth and ribbons, the color of the four directions, and tenderly wrapped it around the scalps for their journey to Sand Creek.

Things were happening more quickly than even Connie imagined. Later, after returning to Denver, Connie removed the

---

[129]The author has personally interviewed all parties involved in this chapter and has been able to verify all of the facts. Tom's real name and the Colorado town in which this incident occurred will remain anonymous. The author doesn't wish to cause any undue publicity for the town or Tom's family. Tom passed away the following November and he is greatly missed by all who knew him.

scalps from the material and gently placed them on her altar. These scalps had belonged to two living people who were slaughtered and they were either Arapaho or Cheyenne. Being an Ojibwa, Connie had no idea what kind of ceremonies should be performed to bury Cheyenne or Arapaho.[130]

The next day she contacted George Tinker, the pastor of the Native American church Connie attended. He in turn contacted Neva Standing Bear Light-In-Lodge. Neva is a Lakota from South Dakota. Many consider her a woman for whom the Lakota spirits watch over. Many times, she has dreamed of the eagles and how they are the spirits of those who had lived before. Neva suggested all involved should participate in a ceremonial sweat lodge so that Connie could go through purification, and guidance for the cere-mony that would be created to take these warriors home. On a warm summer's day they gathered at Tall Bull park in Denver. There was a sense of purpose as each person present focused on the importance of this lodge. George asked Neva to pour water and lead the prayers and songs for the group. The sweat became another mystery for those who attended. For some reason, Connie and Neva both experienced "the hottest sweat" they had ever known. The heat made it almost impossible to breathe, but the hot-ter it got, the more fervent their prayers became. They prayed as they had been directed, for "those who had been killed, those who had killed and for those who would bring these plains warriors home and that the Grandfathers and Grandmothers listen to the pleas of these two leggeds who join their suffering willingly for the People." They then prayed for everything to be done in "a good way, with clean hearts." They had purified themselves for the task at hand.

Connie knew she had one week to make ready for the cere-mony. Many things had to be done as her preparation for the burial ceremony began. There were tobacco ties to be made, sage gath-ered, the feast prepared and the giveaway gifts readied.

Later, during the evening hours, Connie returned home and sat by her altar once again to pray. So much had been understood in the sweat, "that these warriors were no longer strangers, but rela-tions who were to be loved, and cherished." Something seemed terribly odd to Connie as she carefully examined the scalps. They

---

[130]Connie would learn almost a year and a half later that her native Ojibwa people are also Algonquin speaking. She and the Tsis Tsis Tas are related.

had been sewn together as one. The sewing seemed to have been performed by a very dainty hand, probably a woman's, over a century before. Feeling they should be honored as individuals, Connie took out a small sharp knife and gently began separating the two scalps that war and death had bound. As she cut the stitching, an energy, like the underlying current of a massive power plant, replaced her normally tranquil apartment. The movement of these spirits had begun. At first it frightened her, but as Connie cried out she meant no harm, the serge of energy subsided, though it never left her apartment. Connie felt a presence she had never experienced before and she knew she must succeed in her quest.

The following morning Connie decided to make contact with the owner of the land where the massacred occurred, Bill Dawson. In order to hold their ceremony, they needed his permission to enter. After a brief phone conversation with him, she left her apartment and made the two hundred mile journey to Sand Creek to meet with Dawson, a man caught in the controversy of history's continuing drama. After a lengthy conversation with him about her predicament and the decision to bury the scalps, she asked for permission to hold the ceremonies on his land. It didn't take long for him to grant the request. He was convinced of Connie's sincerity, but he also had his own views of what happened at Sand Creek on that November day.[131]

Dawson is a man who easily fits the land and its legacy. He is a cattleman, like those before him who has worked hard to keep this land clean so his cattle will grow healthier and fatter with each new season. But he knows it is also a land on which the vanquished fell one hundred twenty-eight years before. There are those who call what happened here a "battle" and not a massacre, and most people who talk to Dawson about the event misconstrue his views as being bigoted. Bill Dawson is a military history buff who has been in the Army National Guard for twenty-six years. His definition of the word "massacre" is one of the continued causes of debate about what really transpired here so long ago.[132] But Dawson will be one of the first to tell any visitor whatever occurred on this land was a real tragedy. And he also makes it clear, he now owns the land and

---

[131]The author and Mr. Dawson have wide differences of opinion as to what happened at Sand Creek. But the author has found Mr. Dawson to be very thoughtful, hospitable and likeable.

[132]Mr. Dawson's definition of "massacre" is that totally unarmed persons were murdered without any means to defend themselves.

uses it for his purposes. Yet time after time, he has given permission for Native Americans to hold ceremonies here to pray and give respect to the ones who died here. To Dawson, this land is his livelihood and life, but to many Native Americans, his cattle grazing on this land is akin to having those same cattle roam free in Forest Lawn Cemetery.[133]

Connie thanked Bill for his time and permission and returned to Denver. The next weekend Connie Buffalo and her group of eight people returned to fulfill a promise. After a four hour journey from Denver, their vehicles arrived at the site. And, as Sweet Medicine had prophesied hundreds of years before, cattle now graze where buffalo once roamed. Except for barbed-wire fences separating neighboring ranches, this group of people found the land near Big Sandy Creek remarkably desolate. Although deer and antelope can occasionally be found there, far less wildlife roam through the sweet sage and cottonwood tree groves than were present in 1864.

When they arrived at Sand Creek, Connie again met with Bill Dawson, and he showed them where to set up their camp for the night. Their ceremony would begin before the morning star appeared. Neva and the others noticed Big Sandy Creek's bed was now almost dry. Its banks hold just the memory of water that once flowed there in profusion. The darkened sky filled their naked eyes with a myriad of constellations and stars, still unobstructed by the glare of city lights. And on this night a lonely coyote was heard amidst the howl of a tainted wind. Some there said it was the crying of those killed on the 29th November day that blew over the empty plains. Many of those present heard the distinct sounds of "camp noises" coming from an area that held no campsites. The noises Neva and the others heard seemed to have come from another time.

The next morning, long before the sun made its way over the eastern horizon, Neva, Connie and the others made ready for their ceremony. There had been a wind blowing all night and as the ceremony began, as though it were paying respect, the Great-Grandfather's breath stopped breathing, as quiet again filled the morning. Although they had been invited, no Cheyenne or Arapaho were present for this observance. Ancient songs of prayer

---

[133]Again the author wishes to make it clear that Mr. Dawson would never purposely denegrate the Native American's beliefs. I used the analogy of Forest Lawn Cemetery to show the difference in how two races view the land at Sand Creek.

were sung. And prayers were spoken to the Great Wise One Above to give a final resting place to those whose scalps they possessed. The pipe was offered to the four winds, then to the Great One Above and the Great One Below, and tobacco was offered to the spirits of the land.[134] Within a half hour the ceremony was over and the scalps were united with Mother Earth. Connie buried them in a grove of cottonwood trees that formed a circle. As the words of the final prayer began, everyone saw two birds hovering above the circle they had formed for their prayer. The birds remained there during the entire prayer. As the last words of the prayer were uttered, the birds began singing as they flew up towards the sky, vanishing from everyone's view. As they disappeared, the sun's light spread across the land and years. Mother earth awoke in peace from her memories of sadness. Soon song birds filled the countryside around her. They sang a welcome to the day and another chapter had begun.

The land seemed to open itself to Neva's every sense, as though she belonged there. And yet, as far as she knew, none of her people had died at Sand Creek. She was overcome with an overwhelming sense of sorrow for the events which took place there one hundred twenty-seven years before and with a sense of joy she could help those spirits who dwelled upon the land. Four months later, she discovered she was a blood relative of William Bent and Owl Woman.[135]

Connie, too, was moved by this experience. She felt as though the spirits of the two warriors would never be far from those who had fulfilled the request to bring prayer, peace and forgiveness. Although Connie felt she'd lost two friends when the scalps were buried, she was unaware of the profound effect she had made on the people her fateful excursion introduced her to. During her silent communion with the spirits at Sand Creek, her thoughts were never absent from people like Tom. Yet his thoughts were of her as a tranquility set into his life's pattern, wondering but not worrying whether Connie's quest for the burial were successful. Tom's wife later told Connie of how he was more at peace with himself after meeting her. Death called on Tom four months later. He came quietly and serenely to a man who had lived a hard and fast life.

---

[134]Lakota pipe ceremonies differ from the Tsis Tsis Tas in that they pay homage first to the four directions, then to the sky and lastly to the earth.

[135]During the author's interviews with Neva Standing Bear Light-in-the-Lodge and Lucille Bent, the two women discovered they were related to each other through Lucille's Lakota heritage.

Connie's gentle spirit graced this land and touched all those she met. With the ceremony now over, a new quiet rested on the land. Connie, Neva and the others prayed to forgive the perpetrators who committed those terrible deeds on November 29,1864, and prayed for peace for their victims. In the early morning light, Neva heard a faint echo in the prairie as the sun slowly peeked over the horizon. It seemed to reverberate across the blades of grass and sage. It seemed to be the echo of laughing children who are now long gone. But there was also a song heard in the dawning. It was a song written by the hand of prejudice and with the blood of innocents. It was a song composed by the hand of hatred and greed. Its notes were written in tears and shattered promises and its melody was set to tragedy. This is how man defined this song.

But the Creator understood that this song alone demands vengeance and more hatred and is this not the ultimate tragedy? In the summer of 1991 a new melody was brought into being. Its lyrics sang of compassion and wisdom that said: "All come from the Great Spirit and all must be held in forgiveness. You must always remember that good and evil are deep within each heart and no man is separate from his brother. Pray that all hearts come to good."

So now two songs are intertwined at Sand Creek, one of hate and one of forgiveness. And they will forever permeate this land of the Cheyenne and Arapaho.

Bibliography

Ambrose, Stephen E. *Crazy Horse and Custer. (The Parallel Lives of Two American Warriors.)* Meridian Book New American Library, 1975.

Ashley, Susan Riley. "Reminiscences of Colorado in the Early Sixties." *The Colorado Magazine*, Vol. XIII 1936, pp. 219-230.

Anthony, Major Scott J. Letter to his brother Web. *Rocky Mountain News*, Denver, CO, December 1, 1864

Bent, Lucille (Grand daughter of George Bent). Interview, Clinton, OK, 1990, 1991.

Berthrong, Donald J. *The Southern Cheyenne.* Norman, OK: University of Oklahoma Press, 1963.

Berthrong, Donald J. *The Cheyenne and Arapaho Ordeal.* Norman, OK: University of Oklahoma, 1976.

Berthrong, Donald J. Interview, West Lafayette, IN, 1989.

Brown, Dee. *The Fetterman Massacre.* First Bison Book Printing, 1971. (Formerly titled, *Fort Phil Kearny, and American Saga.* Putman, 1962.

Brown, Dee. *Bury My Heart at Wounded Knee.* Holt, Rhinehart and Winston, 1970.

Bull, Richard Tall (A chief of the Northern Cheyenne and oral historian). Denver, CO, 1989.

Campbell, United States Senator Ben Nighthorse (A chief of the Northern Cheyenne). Interview, Durango, CO, 1989, 1990, 1991.

Capps, Benjamin. *The Old West The Indians.* Time-Life Books. Alexandria, VA: Time-Life Books Inc., 1973.

Cardinal, Jack (Mat'O, Shoshoni storyteller). Interview, Thornton, CO, 1989, 1990, 1991.

Carrington, Margaret Irvin. *Absaraka: Home of the Crows.* J.B. Lippincott and Co. Philadelphia, PA., 1868., First Bison Book, 1983.

Colorado Springs Gazette Telegraph, article August 8, 1990.

Craig, Reyinald S. *The Fighting Parson.* Westernlore Press, 1959.

Davis, Burke *The Long Surrender,* Random House, N.Y., 1985.

Grinnell, George B. *The Fighting Cheyennes.* Norman, OK: University of Oklahoma Press, 1915.

Grinnell, George B. *The Cheyenne Indians.* Cooper Square Publishers, Inc., 1962.

Grob, Gerald N. *Mental Institutions in America: Social Policy to 1875.* The Free Press, A Division of MacMillan Publishing Co., Inc. 1973.

Hall, Frank. *History of Colorado.* 1889-1895.

Hanway, Paul (Northern Arapaho). Interview, Denver, CO, 1989, 1990, 1991.

Hoig, Stan. *The Sand Creek Massacre.* Norman, OK: University of Oklahoma Press, 1961.

Hyde, George E. *The Life of George Bent, Written From His Letters.* Norman, OK: University of Oklahoma Press, 1968.

Hyde, George. *Red Cloud's Folk.* Norman, OK: University of Oklahoma Press, 1937.

Joint Committee on the Conduct of the War, Massacre of the Cheyenne Indians, 38th Congress, Second Session. *The Sand Creek Massacre: A Documentary History.* Washington, D.C.: 1865; Report of the Secretary of War, 39th Congress, Second Session. Senate Executive Document No. 26, Washington, D.C.: 1867. Sol Lewis Publisher, 1973.

Karnes, Thomas L. *William Gilpin: Western Nationalist.* University of Texas Press, 1970.

Kelsey, Harry. E. *Frontier Capitalist: The Life of John Evans.* State Historical Society of Colorado and The Pruett Publishing Company, 1969.

Koestler, Frances A. *The Unseen Minority.* The American Foundation for the Blind, Inc. 1976.

Lavender, David. *Bent's Fort.* University of Nebraska Press, 1954.

Leonard, Stephen J. and Thomas J. Noel. *Denver—Mining Camp to Metropolis.* The University Press of Colorado, 1990.

McMechen, E.C. *Life of Governor Evans.* 1924.

Magoffin, Susan. *Down the Santa Fe Trail and Into Mexico The Diary of Susan Magoffin, 1846-1847.* Yale University Press, 1926.

Meyer, Clarence. *American Folk Medicine .*Thomas Y. Crowell Co. Inc. 1973.

Noel, Thomas J. *The City and The Saloon.* University of Nebraska Press, 1982.

Panana, Marcella (Great-great-great granddaughter of Yellow Wolf). Interview, Clinton, OK, 1990, 1991.

Peterson, Dale *A Mad People's History of Madness*, University of Pittsburg Press. 1982.

Pratt, Richard Henry *Battlefield and Classroom Four Decades With The American Indian*, 1867-1904, New Haven & London, Yale University Press, Hartford, Connecticut, 1964.

Prairie, Robert Chief (Southern Cheyenne). Interview, Clinton, OK, 1990, 1991.

Sandoz, Mari *Cheyenne Autumn*, McIntosh and Otis Inc., 1953.

Sawyer, Tom Hayden (Great-great grandson of John Evans). Interview, Evergreen, CO, 1989, 1990, 1991.

Shoup, Colonel George L. Letter to his friend Captain Sopris. *Rocky Mountain News*, Denver, CO, December 7, 1864.

Sipes, Mrs. Cleo, Great-granddaughter of Medicine Water and Buffalo Calf Woman (Mochsi). Interview, Clinton, Oklahoma. August 19, 1992.

Sipes, John L., Great-Great-Grandson of Medicine Water and Mochsi (Buffalo Calf Woman) Historian for the Oklahoma Historic Society. Interview, Clinton, Oklahoma. August 22, 1992, August 24, 1992.

Soule, Silas, Two letters to his mother. December 18, 1864, January 8, 1965.

Stern, Thomas D. "The Controversial Career of Edward W. Wynkoop." *The Colorado Magazine*, 56/1 and 2, 1979.

Strange Owl, Ann (Great-great grand daughter of William Bent and Owl Woman). Interview, Loveland, CO, 1989, 1990, 1991.

Trenholm, Virginia Cole (Lived and worked with the Arapaho and Shoshonis for fifty years). Interview, Cheyenne, WY, 1990, 1991.

Utley, Robert M. *Cavalier In Buckskin*. Norman, OK: University of Oklahoma Press, 1988.

Wilson, Elinor. *Jim Beckwourth, Black Mountain Man, War Chief of the Crows*. Norman, OK: University of Oklahoma Press, 1914.

Wynkoop, Edward W. Unfinished manuscript. Colorado History MSS II-20, Colorado State Historical Society, 28.

NEWSPAPERS

The Miner's Registry, Central City, CO, December 12, 1864.

Rocky Mountain News, Denver, CO,

Beckwourth, James P., April 18, 1860.
Byers, William, December 22, 1864.
Byers, William, December 29, 1864.
Byers, William, December 30, 1864.
Chivington, John M., December 7, 1864.
Evans, John. August 11, 1864.

Author Unknown, December 23, 1864.
Author Unknown, December 24, 1864.
Author Unknown, December 28, 1864.
Author Unknown, December 29, 1864.
Author Unknown, June 9, 1868.
Author Unknown, July 3-7, 1897.
Author Unknown, February 15, 1941.

The Denver Republican, Denver, CO, July 3, 1897, October 5, 1894.

Index

Patrick M. Mendoza

For the past seventeen years Patrick Mendoza has made his living as a professional storyteller and singer. He is a Vietnam veteran and has been a policeman, bounty hunter (for two weeks), professional diver, martial arts instructor (he holds black belts in Tae kwon do and a form of kung fu), power lifter, photographer, composer and is an adopted Cheyenne (honorary).

He has toured all over the United States as well as England, Ireland, Scotland, Wales, Canada and Mexico, thrilling audiences, both young and old, with his songs and tales of Americana. For the past seven years he has spent hundreds of hours in historic societies, libraries and museums researching the material for this, his first book, and by living and visiting with many of the descendants of the victims and perpetrators of Sand Creek's tragedy. On November of 1993 his folk opera, "Song of the Plains," based on this book, will premier at the Arvada Center for the Performing Arts in Arvada, Colorado.